FIX-IT and FORGET-IT®

INSTANT POT®
COMFORT FOOD

Fix-It and Forget-It®
INSTANT POT®
COMFORT
FOOD

100 Crowd-Pleasing Recipes

HOPE COMERFORD
Photos by Bonnie Matthews

New York, New York

Good Books books may be purchased in bulk at special discounts for sales promotion, corporate gifts, fund-raising, or educational purposes. Special editions can also be created to specifications. For details, contact the Special Sales Department, Good Books, 307 West 36th Street, 11th Floor, New York, NY 10018 or info@skyhorsepublishing.com.

Good Books is an imprint of Skyhorse Publishing, Inc.®, a Delaware corporation.

Visit our website at www.goodbooks.com.

10 9 8 7 6 5 4 3 2 1

Library of Congress Cataloging-in-Publication Data

Names: Comerford, Hope, author. | Matthews, Bonnie, photographer.
Title: Fix-it and forget-it Instant Pot comfort food : 100 crowd-pleasing
   recipes / Hope Comerford ; photos by Bonnie Matthews.
Description: New York, New York : Good Books, [2023] | Series: Fix-it and
   forget-it | Includes index. | Summary: "100 delicious and satisfying
   dishes you can whip up in your Instant Pot"—Provided by publisher.
Identifiers: LCCN 2022054636 (print) | LCCN 2022054637 (ebook) | ISBN
   9781680998634 (paperback) | ISBN 9781680998788 (epub)
Subjects: LCSH: Smart cookers. | Comfort food. | Quick and easy cooking. |
   One-dish meals. | LCGFT: Cookbooks.
Classification: LCC TX840.S63 C6524 2023 (print) | LCC TX840.S63 (ebook)
   | DDC 641.5/87—dc23/eng/20221121
LC record available at https://lccn.loc.gov/2022054636
LC ebook record available at https://lccn.loc.gov/2022054637

Cover design by David Ter-Avanesyan
Cover photo by Bonnie Matthews

Print ISBN: 978-1-68099-863-4
Ebook ISBN: 978-1-68099-878-8

Printed in China

Contents

Welcome to Fix-It and Forget-It Instant Pot Comfort Food

What sorts of foods come to mind when you think about "comfort foods"? Maybe a steaming bowl of chicken noodle soup, a bubbling pot of chili, or a generous serving of creamy macaroni and cheese. In these pages, you're sure to find some of your go-to comfort foods as well as some new-to-you dishes that might just become your new favorites! This book is stuffed with 100 of the best comforting Instant Pot recipes around. Best of all, these recipes come straight from the Fix-It and Forget-It community, which we all know and love.

You'll find tried-and-true comfort food recipes like Chicken and Dumplings, Spaghetti and Meatballs, Pot Roast, Lasagna, Beef Stew, Mashed Potatoes, Biscuits and Gravy, Strawberry Shortcake, Quick and Yummy Peach Cobbler, and *so* much more all right here in this book, all designed for the Instant Pot. Take the guesswork out of your weekly "what's for dinner?" and plan your comforting meals from this amazing collection of 100 crowd-pleasing recipes.

What Is an Instant Pot?

In short, an Instant Pot is a digital pressure cooker that also has multiple other functions. Not only can it be used as a pressure cooker, but depending on which model Instant Pot you have, you can set it to do things like sauté, cook rice, grains, porridge, soup/stew, beans/chili, porridge, meat, poultry, cake, eggs, and yogurt. You can use the Instant Pot to steam or slow cook or even set it manually. Because the Instant Pot has so many functions, it takes away the need for multiple appliances on your counter and allows you to use fewer pots and pans.

Getting Started with Your Instant Pot

Get to Know Your Instant Pot . . .

The very first thing most Instant Pot owners do is called the water test. It helps you get to know your Instant Pot a bit, familiarizes you with it, and might even take a bit of your apprehension away (because if you're anything like me, I was scared to death to use it).

Step 1: Plug in your Instant Pot. This may seem obvious to some, but when we're nervous about using a new appliance, sometimes we forget things like this.

Step 2: Make sure the inner pot is inserted in the cooker. You should *never* attempt to cook anything in your device without the inner pot, or you will ruin your Instant Pot. Food should never come into contact with the actual housing unit.

Step 3: The inner pot has lines for each cup. Fill the inner pot with water until it reaches the 3-cup line.

Step 4: Check the sealing ring to be sure it's secure and in place. You should not be able to move it around. If it's not in place properly, you may experience issues with the pot letting out a lot of steam while cooking, or not coming to pressure.

Step 5: Seal the lid. There is an arrow on the lid between and "open" and "close." There is also an arrow on the top of the base of the Instant Pot between a picture of a locked lock and an unlocked lock. Line those arrows up, then turn the lid toward the picture of the lock (left).You will hear a noise that will indicate the lid is locked. If you do not hear a noise, it's not locked. Try it again.

Step 6: *Always* check to see if the steam valve on top of the lid is turned to "sealing." If it's not on "sealing" and is on "venting," it will not be able to come to pressure.

Step 7: Press the Steam button and use the +/- arrow to set it to 2 minutes. Once it's at the desired time, you don't need to press anything else. In a few seconds, the Instant Pot will begin all on its own. For those of us with digital slow cookers, we have a tendency to look for the "start" button, but there isn't one on the Instant Pot.

Step 8: Now you wait for the "magic" to happen! The cooking will begin once the device comes to pressure. This can take anywhere from 5 to 30 minutes, in my experience. Then, you will see the countdown happen (from the time you set it for). After that, the Instant Pot will beep, which means your meal is done!

Step 9: Your Instant Pot will now automatically switch to "warm" and begin a count of how many minutes it's been on warm. The next part is where you either wait for the NPR, or natural pressure release (the pressure releases on its own) or do what's called a QR, or quick release (you manually release the pressure). Which method you choose depends on what you're cooking, but in this case, you can choose either, because it's just water. For NPR, you will wait for the lever to move all the way back over to "venting" and watch the pinion (float valve) next to the lever. It will be flush with the lid when at full pressure and will drop when the pressure is done releasing. If you choose QR, be very careful not to have your hands over the vent, as the steam is very hot and you can burn yourself.

The Three Most Important Buttons You Need to Know About

You will find the majority of recipes will use the following three buttons:

Manual/Pressure Cook: Some older models tend to say "Manual," and the newer models seem to say "Pressure Cook." They mean the same thing. From here, you use the +/- button to change the cook time. After several seconds, the Instant Pot will begin its process. The exact name of this button will vary on your model of Instant Pot.

Sauté: Many recipes will have you sauté vegetables, or brown meat before beginning the pressure cooking process. For this setting, you will not use the lid of the Instant Pot.

Keep Warm/Cancel: This may just be the most important button on the Instant Pot. When you forget to use the +/- buttons to change the time for a recipe, or you press a wrong button, you can hit Keep Warm/Cancel and it will turn your Instant Pot off for you.

What Do All the Buttons Do?

With so many buttons, it's hard to remember what each one does or means. You can use this as a quick guide in a pinch.

Soup/Broth. This button cooks at high pressure for 30 minutes. It can be adjusted using the +/- buttons to cook more, for 40 minutes, or less, for 20 minutes.

Meat/Stew. This button cooks at high pressure for 35 minutes. It can be adjusted using the +/- buttons to cook more, for 45 minutes, or less, for 20 minutes.

Bean/Chili. This button cooks at high pressure for 30 minutes. It can be adjusted using the +/- buttons to cook more, for 40 minutes, or less, for 25 minutes.

Poultry. This button cooks at high pressure for 15 minutes. It can be adjusted using the +/- buttons to cook more, for 30 minutes, or less, for 5 minutes.

Rice. This button cooks at low pressure and is the only fully automatic program. It is for cooking white rice and will automatically adjust the cooking time depending on the amount of water and rice in the cooking pot.

Multigrain. This button cooks at high pressure for 40 minutes. It can be adjusted using the +/- buttons to cook more, for 45 minutes of warm water soaking time and 60 minutes pressure cooking time, or less, for 20 minutes.

Porridge. This button cooks at high pressure for 20 minutes. It can be adjusted using the +/- buttons to cook more, for 30 minutes, or less, for 15 minutes.

Steam. This button cooks at high pressure for 10 minutes. It can be adjusted using the +/- buttons to cook more, for 15 minutes, or less, for 3 minutes. Always use a rack or steamer basket with this function, because it heats at full power continuously while it's coming to pressure, and you do not want food in direct contact with the bottom of the pressure cooking pot or it will burn. Once it reaches pressure, the Steam button regulates pressure by cycling on and off, similar to the other pressure buttons.

Less | Normal | More. Adjust between the *Less | Normal | More* settings by pressing the same cooking function button repeatedly until you get to the desired setting. (Older versions use the *Adjust* button.)

+/- Buttons. Adjust the cook time up [+] or down [-]. (On newer models, you can also press and hold [-] or [+] for 3 seconds to turn sound OFF or ON.)

Cake. This button cooks at high pressure for 30 minutes. It can be adjusted using the +/- buttons to cook more, for 40 minutes, or less, for 25 minutes.

Egg. This button cooks at high pressure for 5 minutes. It can be adjusted using the +/- buttons to cook more, for 6 minutes, or less, for 4 minutes.

Instant Pot Tips and Tricks and Other Things You May Not Know

- Never attempt to cook directly in the Instant Pot without the inner pot!

- Once you set the time, you can walk away. It will show the time you set it to, then will change to the word "on" while the pressure builds. Once the Instant Pot has come to pressure, you will once again see the time you set it for. It will count down from there.

- Always make sure the sealing ring is securely in place. If it shows signs of wear or tear, it needs to be replaced.

- Have a sealing ring for savory recipes and a separate sealing ring for sweet recipes. Many people report their desserts tasting like a roast (or another savory food) if they try to use the same sealing ring for all recipes.

- The stainless steel rack (trivet) the Instant Pot comes with can used to keep food from being completely submerged in liquid, like baked potatoes or ground beef. It can also be used to set another pot on, for pot-in-pot cooking.

- If you use warm or hot liquid instead of cold liquid, you may need to adjust the cooking time, or the food may not come out done.

- Always double-check to see that the valve on the lid is set to "sealing" and not "venting" when you first lock the lid. This will save you from the Instant Pot not coming to pressure.

- Use Natural Pressure Release for tougher cuts of meat, recipes with high starch (like rice or grains), and recipes with a high volume of liquid. This means you let the Instant Pot naturally release pressure. The little bobbin will fall once pressure is released completely.

- Use Quick Release for more delicate cuts of meat, such as seafood and chicken breasts, and for steaming vegetables. This means you manually turn the vent (being careful not to put your hand over the vent) to release the pressure. The little bobbin will fall once pressure is released completely.

- Make sure there is a clear pathway for the steam to release. The last thing you want is to ruin the bottom of your cupboards with all that steam.

- You *must* use liquid in the Instant Pot. The *minimum* amount of liquid you should have in the inner pot is ½ cup, but most recipes work best with at least 1 cup.

- Do *not* overfill the Instant Pot! It should only be ½ full for rice or beans (food that expands greatly when cooked), or ⅔ of the way full for almost everything else. Do not fill it to the max fill line.

- In this book, the Cook Time *does not* take into account the amount of time it will take the Instant Pot to come to pressure, or the amount of time it will take the Instant Pot to release pressure. Be aware of this when choosing a recipe to make.

- If the Instant Pot is not coming to pressure, it's usually because the sealing ring is not on properly, or the vent is not set to "sealing."
- The more liquid, or the colder the ingredients, the longer it will take for the Instant Pot to come to pressure.
- Always make sure that the Instant Pot is dry before inserting the inner pot, and make sure the inner pot is dry before inserting it into the Instant Pot.
- Use a binder clip to hold the inner pot tight against the outer pot when sautéing and stirring. This will keep the pot from "spinning" in the base.
- Doubling a recipe does not change the cook time, but instead it will take longer to come up to pressure.
- You do not always need to double the liquid when doubling a recipe. Depending on what you're making, more liquid may make the food too watery. Use your best judgment.
- When using the slow cooker function, use the following chart:

Slow Cooker	Instant Pot
Warm	Less or Low
Low	Normal or Medium
High	More or High

Instant Pot Accessories

Most Instant Pots come with a stainless steel trivet. Below, you will find a list of accessories that will be used in this cookbook. Most of these accessories can be purchased in-store or online.

- Trivet and/or steamer basket—stainless steel or silicone
- 7-inch nonstick springform cake pan
- 7-inch round baking pan
- 7-inch Bundt cake pan
- Sling or trivet with handles
- 1½-quart round baking dish
- Silicone egg bite molds

Breakfasts

Cinnamon Caramel Coffee Cake

Hope Comerford, Clinton Township, MI

Makes 4 servings
Prep. Time: 10 minutes *Cooking Time: 20 minutes*

Topping:

½ cup all-purpose flour

⅓ cup brown sugar

½ tsp. cinnamon

2 Tbsp. cold butter, chopped

¼ cup chopped pecans, *optional*

Batter:

2 cups all-purpose flour

1 tsp. baking powder

⅓ cup brown sugar

1 tsp. cinnamon

1 tsp. vanilla extract

¼ tsp. salt

2 Tbsp. butter, melted

⅔ cup milk

½ cup caramel bits

1 cup water

1. Spray a 7-inch springform pan with nonstick spray.

2. Mix the flour, brown sugar, cinnamon, and cold butter from the toppings list with a fork, pastry cutter, or with clean fingers. Add in the optional chopped pecans if desired.

3. Spread half of the topping in the springform pan. Set the rest aside.

4. Mix the batter ingredients in a bowl and stir until smooth.

5. Pour half the batter into the pan. Sprinkle the remaining topping over the batter, then pour the remaining batter over the top.

6. Cover the pan with foil.

7. Pour the water into the inner pot of the Instant Pot and place the trivet inside. Make sure the handles are up.

8. Place the covered springform pan on top of the trivet.

9. Seal the lid and set the vent to sealing.

10. Manually set the cook time for 20 minutes.

11. When cook time is up, let the pressure release naturally, then carefully remove the lid and pan.

12. Let the cake cool with the foil off before slicing and serving.

Quick and Easy Instant Pot Cinnamon Rolls

Hope Comerford, Clinton Township, MI

Makes 5 servings
Prep. Time: 5 minutes ❧ Cooking Time: 13 minutes

2 cups water

17-oz. can Pillsbury Grands!™ Cinnamon Rolls with Original Icing

1. Place the water in the inner pot of the Instant Pot, then place the trivet inside.

2. Cover the trivet with aluminum foil so that it also wraps up the sides.

3. Grease a 7-inch round pan and arrange the cinnamon rolls inside. Set the icing aside. Place this pan on top of the aluminum foil inside the inner pot.

4. Secure the lid and make sure the vent is in the sealed position. Press Manual, high pressure for 13 minutes.

5. Release the pressure manually when cooking time is up.

6. Remove the lid carefully so that the moisture does not drip on the cinnamon rolls.

7. Drizzle the icing on top of the cinnamon rolls and serve.

Cinnamon French Toast Casserole

Hope Comerford, Clinton Township, MI

Makes 8 servings
Prep. Time: 10 minutes ⚬ *Cooking Time: 20 minutes*

3 eggs

2 cups milk

¼ cup maple syrup

I tsp. vanilla extract

I tsp. cinnamon

Pinch salt

16-oz. loaf cinnamon swirl bread, cubed and left out overnight to go stale

Nonstick cooking spray

I cup water

Serving suggestion:
Serve with whipped cream and fresh fruit on top, with an extra sprinkle of cinnamon.

1. In a medium bowl, whisk together the eggs, milk, maple syrup, vanilla, cinnamon, and salt. Stir in the cubes of cinnamon swirl bread.

2. You will need a 7-inch round pan for this. Spray the inside with nonstick cooking spray, then pour the bread mixture into the pan.

3. Place the trivet in the bottom of the inner pot, then pour in the water.

4. Make a foil sling and insert it onto the trivet. Carefully place the 7-inch pan on top of the foil sling/trivet.

5. Secure the lid to the locked position, then make sure the vent is turned to sealing.

6. Press the Manual button and use the "+/-" button to set the Instant Pot for 20 minutes.

7. When the cook time is over, let the Instant Pot release naturally for 5 minutes, then quick release the rest.

Giant Healthy Pancake

Hope Comerford, Clinton Township, MI

Makes 4 servings
Prep. Time: 10 minutes ⚹ *Cooking Time: 17 minutes*

¾ cup whole wheat flour

¼ cup all-purpose flour

¾ tsp. baking powder

¾ tsp. baking soda

I large egg

I ¼ cups unsweetened almond milk

I ½ Tbsp. unsweetened applesauce

Nonstick cooking spray

I cup water

Serving suggestion:
Serve with maple syrup, a drizzle of honey, or topped with your favorite fruit.

1. In a bowl, mix the whole wheat flour, all-purpose flour, baking powder, and baking soda.

2. In a smaller bowl, mix the egg, milk, and unsweetened applesauce until well combined. Pour into the dry ingredients and stir until well combined.

3. Spray a 7-inch round springform pan with nonstick cooking spray and then pour the pancake batter into it.

4. Pour the water into the inner pot of the Instant Pot. Place the springform pan on the trivet and carefully lower the trivet into the inner pot.

5. Secure the lid and make sure the vent is set to sealing.

6. Manually set your Instant Pot to Low pressure and set the cook time for 17 minutes.

7. When the cook time is over, manually release the pressure.

8. Remove the lid and carefully lift the trivet out with oven mitts.

9. Remove the cake from the pan and allow to cool for a few minutes before serving and to allow the moisture on the surface of the cake to dry.

Biscuits and Gravy the Instant Pot Way

Hope Comerford, Clinton Township, MI

Makes 4 servings
Prep. Time: 5 minutes ⚸ Cooking Time: 16–20 minutes

Gravy:
1 Tbsp. butter
8 oz. bulk breakfast sausage
3 Tbsp. flour
½ tsp. garlic powder
¼ tsp. sea salt
¼ tsp. black pepper
1½ cups milk

Biscuits:
¾ cups baking mix
⅓ cup milk
¼ tsp. black pepper
¼ tsp. sea salt

1. Set the Instant Pot to the Sauté setting and place the butter in the inner pot to melt.

2. Add in the breakfast sausage and sauté until browned, about 8 minutes.

3. Stir in the flour, garlic powder, sea salt, and pepper.

4. Whisk in the milk, and bring to a simmer, stirring occasionally.

5. Press Cancel on the Instant Pot.

6. In a bowl, mix the biscuit ingredients.

7. Place dollops of the biscuit mixture over the gravy.

8. Secure the lid and set the vent to sealing.

9. Manually set the cook time for 4 minutes.

10. When cook time is up, let the pressure release naturally for 5 minutes, then manually release the remaining pressure.

11. Serve and enjoy!

Breakfast Burrito Casserole

Hope Comerford, Clinton Township, MI

Makes 6 burritos
Prep. Time: 5–7 minutes   Cooking Time: 13 minutes

1 tsp. olive oil

8 oz. ground chorizo

⅓ cup chopped onion

1 poblano pepper, seeded and diced

16 oz. frozen diced potatoes

1 cup, plus 1 Tbsp. water, *divided*

4 eggs

¼ tsp. salt

¼ tsp. pepper

⅓ cup shredded Mexican blend cheese (or any cheese of your liking)

¼ cup of your favorite salsa, *optional*

6 flour tortillas

1. Set the Instant Pot to the Sauté function and heat the olive oil.

2. Add in the chorizo, onion, and poblano pepper, and sauté until browned, about 5 minutes.

3. Add in the potatoes and sauté for about 5 minutes longer.

4. Remove the chorizo/potato mix from the inner pot and set aside.

5. Pour 1 cup of water into the inner pot and scrape up any bits on the bottom of the pot.

6. Place the trivet with handles into the inner pot.

7. In a bowl, mix the eggs, tablespoon of water, salt, and pepper. Stir in the chorizo/potato mix.

8. Spray a 7-inch round baking pan with nonstick spray. Pour the egg/chorizo, potato mix into the pan and sprinkle with the cheese. Cover with foil.

9. Place the pan on top of the trivet. Secure the lid and set the vent to sealing.

10. Manually set the cook time for 13 minutes on high pressure.

11. When cook time is up, let the pressure release naturally.

12. When the pin drops, remove the lid and then carefully remove the baking pan from the trivet.

13. Fill the tortillas with some of the filling and wrap up like a burrito.

Southwestern Egg Casserole

Eileen Eash, Lafayette, CO

Makes 12 servings
Prep. Time: 10 minutes ☙ *Cooking Time: 20 minutes*

1 cup water
2½ cups egg substitute
½ cup flour
1 teaspoon baking powder
⅛ tsp. salt
⅛ tsp. pepper
2 cups cottage cheese
1½ cups shredded sharp cheddar cheese
¼ cup margarine, melted
2 (4-oz.) cans chopped green chilies

1. Place the steaming rack into the bottom of the inner pot and pour in 1 cup of water.

2. Grease a round 7-inch springform pan.

3. Combine the egg substitute, flour, baking powder, salt, and pepper in a mixing bowl. It will be lumpy.

4. Stir in the cheeses, margarine, and green chilies then pour into the springform pan.

5. Place the springform pan onto the steaming rack, close the lid, and secure to the locking position. Be sure the vent is turned to sealing. Manually set the cook time for 20 minutes on high pressure.

6. When cook time is up, let the pressure release naturally.

7. Carefully remove the springform pan with the handles of the steaming rack and allow to stand 10 minutes before cutting and serving.

Potato-Bacon Gratin

Valerie Drobel, Carlisle, PA

Makes 8 (5-oz.) servings
Prep. Time: 20 minutes   ☙   Cooking Time: 40 minutes

1 Tbsp. olive oil

6-oz. bag fresh spinach

1 clove garlic, minced

4 large potatoes, peeled or unpeeled, *divided*

Nonstick cooking spray

6 oz. Canadian bacon slices, *divided*

5 oz. grated Swiss cheddar, *divided*

1 cup chicken broth

1. Set the Instant Pot to Sauté and pour in the olive oil. Cook the spinach and garlic in olive oil just until spinach is wilted (5 minutes or less). Press Cancel.

2. Cut potatoes into thin slices about ¼-inch thick.

3. Spray a 7-inch springform pan with nonstick spray, then layer ⅓ the potatoes, half the bacon, ⅓ the cheese, and half the wilted spinach.

4. Repeat layers ending with potatoes. Reserve ⅓ cheese for later.

5. Pour chicken broth over all.

6. Wipe the bottom of the inner pot to soak up any remaining oil, then add in 2 cups of water and the steaming rack. Place the springform pan on top.

7. Close the lid and secure to the locking position. Be sure the vent is turned to sealing. Manually set the cook time for 35 minutes on high pressure.

8. When cook time is up, manually release the pressure.

9. Top with the remaining cheese, then allow to stand 10 minutes before removing from the Instant Pot, cutting, and serving.

Appetizers

Queso Dip

Hope Comerford, Clinton Township, MI

Makes 10 servings

Prep. time: 5 minutes   Cooking Time: 18 minutes

1 tsp. olive oil

½ cup chopped onion

4 cloves garlic, minced

1 cup water

2-lb. block of Velveeta Queso Blanco, chopped into chunks

8-oz. block cream cheese, chopped into chunks

2 (10-oz.) cans Ro-Tel Diced Tomatoes with Green Chilies

1. Set the Instant Pot to the Sauté function and add the oil to heat.

2. Sauté the onion and garlic for about 3 minutes. Place it in a 7-cup oven-safe glass bowl.

3. Pour the cup of water into the bottom of the inner pot and scrape any bits off the bottom. Press Cancel.

4. Add the remaining ingredients to the glass bowl. Cover completely with foil.

5. Place the trivet with handles into the Inner Pot, then place the covered bowl on the trivet.

6. Secure the lid and set the vent to sealing.

7. Manually set the cook time for 18 minutes on high pressure.

8. When cook time is up, manually release the pressure.

9. When the pin drops, remove the lid and carefully remove the glass covered dish from the inner pot. Remove the foil and whisk until smooth.

Instant Pot Chicken Nachos

Hope Comerford, Clinton Township, MI

Makes 6 servings
Prep. Time: 5 minutes 　　 Cooking Time: 20 minutes

3 lb. boneless skinless chicken breast

1 cup of your favorite salsa

1.25-oz. pkg. taco seasoning

½ cup chicken stock

¼ cup lime juice

12 oz. tortilla chips

1 cup diced onion

½ cup sliced black olives

½ cup chopped tomatoes

¼ cup sliced jalapeños

2 cups shredded cheddar cheese

1 cup shredded lettuce

Serving suggestion:
Serve with sour cream, salsa, and guacamole if you'd like!

1. Place the chicken, salsa, taco seasoning, chicken stock, and lime juice into the inner pot of the Instant Pot.

2. Secure the lid and set the vent to sealing.

3. Manually set the cook time for 10 minutes on high pressure.

4. Preheat the oven to 400°F.

5. When cook time is up, manually release the pressure.

6. When the pin drops, carefully remove the lid. Using a hand mixer, shred the chicken in the pot.

7. Spray a baking sheet with nonstick spray, then spread the tortilla chips over the top.

8. Spread the shredded chicken evenly over the chips, as well as the diced onion, black olives, tomatoes, jalapeño slices, and cheddar cheese.

9. Bake in the oven for about 10 minutes, or until the cheese is melted.

10. Remove from the oven and top with the shredded lettuce.

Buffalo Chicken Dip

Hope Comerford, Clinton Township, MI

Makes 26 servings, about 2 Tbsp./serving
Prep. Time: 15 minutes   Cooking Time: 15 minutes

2 large frozen boneless skinless chicken breasts

¾ cup Frank's RedHot® Original Cayenne Pepper Sauce

½ cup sodium-free chicken broth

1 cup light ranch dressing

2 (8-oz.) packages cream cheese, softened

1½ cups shredded cheddar jack cheese

1. Place the frozen chicken, hot sauce, and chicken broth into the inner pot of the Instant Pot. Secure the lid and make sure the vent is set to sealing.

2. Manually set the cook time for 10 minutes on high pressure. When cooking time is over, let the pressure release naturally for 10 minutes and then manually release the remaining pressure.

3. Remove the lid and press Cancel, then press Sauté.

4. Stir in the ranch dressing, cream cheese, and cheddar jack cheese. Cook, stirring until well blended and warm.

Creamy Spinach Dip

Jessica Stoner, Arlington, OH

Makes 10–12 servings
Prep. Time: 10–15 minutes   ⚜   Cooking Time: 5 minutes

8 oz. cream cheese

1 cup sour cream

½ cup finely chopped onion

½ cup vegetable broth

5 cloves garlic, minced

½ tsp. salt

¼ tsp. black pepper

10 oz. frozen spinach

12 oz. shredded Monterey Jack cheese

12 oz. shredded Parmesan cheese

1. Add cream cheese, sour cream, onion, vegetable broth, garlic, salt, pepper, and spinach to the inner pot of the Instant Pot.

2. Secure lid, make sure vent is set to sealing, and set to the Bean/Chili setting on high pressure for 5 minutes.

3. When cook time is up, manually release the pressure.

4. Add the cheeses and mix well until creamy and well combined.

Serving suggestion:
Serve with whole-grain tortilla chips or whole-grain bread.

Hope's Family Hummus

Hope Comerford, Clinton Township, MI

Makes 24 servings; about 2 Tbsp./serving

Soaking Time: 8 hours, or overnight   ⚘   Prep. Time: 15 minutes   ⚘   Cooking Time: 25 minutes

16-oz. bag dried garbanzo beans, soaked overnight

12 cups water

3 Tbsp. tahini

¼–½ cup lemon juice (depending on your taste)

1 clove garlic

⅛ tsp. cumin

⅛ tsp. salt

¼ cup extra-virgin olive oil, *optional*

Serving suggestion:
My favorite way to serve this is with fresh carrot sticks!

1. Place the garbanzo beans that were soaked overnight into the inner pot of the Instant Pot. Pour in the water.

2. Secure the lid and set the vent to sealing.

3. Manually set the cook time to 25 minutes on high pressure.

4. When the cooking time is over, let the pressure release naturally. This will take around half an hour.

5. Drain off any liquid. Pour the beans into a food processor.

6. When the pin drops, remove the lid. Carefully remove the inner pot and drain the liquid from the beans.

7. Add the tahini, lemon juice, garlic, cumin, and salt into the beans in the food processor and add water so that it reaches just below the level of the beans. Note: If you're unsure of how much lemon juice you want to add, start with less, taste, and add more if you desire. Blend until smooth.

8. Place the hummus in a serving dish. Drizzle with the olive oil if you choose.

Insta Popcorn

Hope Comerford, Clinton Township, MI

Makes 5–6 servings
Prep. Time: 1 minute ⚶ *Cooking Time: about 5 minutes*

2 Tbsp. coconut oil

½ cup popcorn kernels

¼ cup butter, melted, *optional*

Sea salt to taste

1. Set the Instant Pot to Sauté.

2. Melt the coconut oil in the inner pot, then add the popcorn kernels and stir.

3. Press Adjust to bring the temperature up to high.

4. When the corn starts popping, secure the lid on the Instant Pot.

5. When you no longer hear popping, turn off the Instant Pot, remove the lid, and pour the popcorn into a bowl.

6. Top with the optional melted butter and season the popcorn with sea salt to your liking.

Soups, Stews & Chilies

Instantly Good Beef Stew

Hope Comerford, Clinton Township, MI

Makes 6 servings
Prep. Time: 20 minutes & Cooking Time: 35 minutes

3 Tbsp. olive oil, *divided*

2 lb. stewing beef, cubed, *divided*

2 cloves garlic, minced

1 large onion, chopped

3 ribs celery, sliced

3 large potatoes, cubed

2–3 carrots, sliced

8 oz. tomato sauce

10 oz. beef broth

2 tsp. Worcestershire sauce

¼ tsp. pepper

1 bay leaf

Note:

If you want the stew to be a bit thicker, remove some of the potatoes, mash, then stir them back through the stew.

1. Set the Instant Pot to the Sauté function, then add 1 Tbsp. of the oil. Add ⅓ of the beef cubes and brown and sear all sides. Repeat this process twice more with the remaining oil and beef cubes. Set the beef aside.

2. Place the garlic, onion, and celery into the pot and sauté for a few minutes. Press Cancel.

3. Add the beef back in as well as all the remaining ingredients.

4. Secure the lid and make sure the vent is set to sealing. Choose Manual for 35 minutes.

5. When the cook time is over, let the pressure release naturally for 15 minutes, then release any remaining pressure manually.

6. Remove the lid, remove the bay leaf, then serve.

Chill-ay a là Mamma Ree

Maria Shevlin, Sicklerville, NJ

Makes 4–6 servings
Prep. Time: 5 minutes ⚬ Cooking Time: 31–33 minutes

1 Tbsp. olive oil

3–5 cloves garlic, minced

1 cup diced celery

1½ cups diced onion

1½ lb. ground beef

1 lb. sirloin steak, cut into small cubes

1 Tbsp. parsley flakes

1 tsp. garlic powder

1 tsp. onion powder

1 tsp. cumin

1 tsp. oregano

½ tsp. pink salt

½ tsp. black pepper

¼–½ tsp. chili powder

1½ cups chicken or beef stock

1 cup canned petite diced tomatoes

¼ cup hot sauce

2 Tbsp. Worcestershire sauce

1 cup potatoes, peeled and diced

1. Set the Instant Pot to Sauté mode, then add the olive oil, garlic, celery, and onion. Cook until onions and celery are just fork tender, about 3–5 minutes.

2. Add in the ground beef and cubed sirloin. Cook for about 8 minutes, or until about cooked.

3. Add the parsley flakes, garlic powder, onion powder, cumin, oregano, salt, pepper, and chili powder. Stir to combine.

4. Pour in the stock, and stir.

5. Add in the petite diced tomatoes, hot sauce, Worcestershire sauce, and potatoes.

6. Secure the lid and set the vent to sealing. Set the cook time for 20 minutes on high pressure.

7. When cook time is up, let the pressure naturally release.

Serving suggestion:

Serve with sour cream, avocado, cheese, green onion, and lime wedges, and tortilla strips or corn chips for crunch.

Beef Mushroom Barley Soup

Becky Frey, Lebanon, PA

Makes 8 servings

Prep. Time: 20 minutes ⚜ Cooking Time: 25 minutes

2 Tbsp. olive oil, *divided*

I lb. boneless beef chuck, cubed

I large onion, chopped

2 cloves garlic, crushed

I lb. fresh mushrooms, sliced

I celery rib, sliced

2 carrots, sliced

½ tsp. dried thyme, *optional*

8 cups low-sodium beef stock

½ cup uncooked pearl barley

½ tsp. freshly ground pepper

3 Tbsp. chopped fresh parsley

1. Set the Instant Pot to the Sauté function and heat 1 Tbsp. of the olive oil in the inner pot.

2. Brown the beef, in batches if needed, and then remove and set aside.

3. Add the remaining Tbsp. of olive oil and sauté the onion, garlic, and mushrooms for 3 to 4 minutes.

4. Add the beef back in, as well as all the remaining ingredients, except for the parsley. Press Cancel.

5. Secure the lid and set the vent to sealing.

6. Manually set the cook time to 25 minutes on high pressure.

7. When the cooking time is over, let the pressure release naturally for 15 minutes, then manually release the remaining pressure.

8. When the pin drops, remove the lid and stir. Serve each bowl topped with some fresh chopped parsley.

Nancy's Vegetable Beef Soup

Nancy Graves, Manhattan, KS

Makes 8 servings
Prep. Time: 25 minutes ☙ *Cooking Time: 8 hours*

2-lb. roast, cubed, or 2 lb. stewing meat
15-oz. can corn
15-oz. can green beans
1-lb. bag frozen peas
40-oz. can stewed tomatoes
5 tsp. beef bouillon powder
Tabasco to taste
½ tsp. salt

1. Combine all ingredients in the Instant Pot. Do not drain vegetables.

2. Add water to fill inner pot only to the fill line.

3. Secure the lid, or use the glass lid and set the Instant Pot on Slow Cooker Mode, Low, for 8 hours, or until meat is tender and vegetables are soft.

Chicken Noodle Soup

Colleen Heatwole, Burton, MI

Makes 6–8 servings
Prep. Time: 15 minutes   Cooking Time: 4 minutes

2 Tbsp. butter

1 Tbsp. oil

1 medium onion, diced

2 large carrots, diced

3 celery stalks, diced

Salt to taste

3 cloves garlic, minced

1 tsp. thyme

1 tsp. oregano

1 tsp. basil

8 cups chicken broth

2 cups cubed cooked chicken

8 oz. medium egg noodles

1 cup peas (if frozen, thaw while preparing soup)

Pepper to taste

1. In the inner pot of the Instant Pot, melt the butter with oil on the Sauté function.

2. Add the onion, carrots, and celery with a large pinch of salt and continue cooking on Sauté until soft, about 5 minutes, stirring frequently.

3. Add the garlic, thyme, oregano, and basil and sauté an additional minute.

4. Add the broth, cooked chicken, and noodles, stirring to combine all ingredients.

5. Put the lid on the Instant Pot and set the vent to sealing. Manually set the cook time for 4 minutes on high pressure.

6. When time is up, manually release the pressure.

7. When the pin drops, remove the lid and add the thawed peas, stir, adjust seasoning with salt and pepper, and serve.

Chicken Vegetable Soup

Maria Shevlin, Sicklerville, NJ

Makes 6 servings
Prep. Time: 12–25 minutes   *Cooking Time: 4 minutes*

1–2 raw chicken breasts, cubed
½ medium onion, chopped
4 cloves garlic, minced
½ sweet potato, small cubes
1 large carrot, peeled and cubed
4 stalks celery, chopped, leaves included
½ cup frozen corn
¼ cup frozen peas
¼ cup frozen lima beans
1 cup frozen green beans (bite size)
¼–½ cup chopped savoy cabbage
14½-oz. can petite diced tomatoes
3 cups chicken bone broth
1 tsp. salt
½ tsp. black pepper
1 tsp. garlic powder
¼ cup chopped fresh parsley
¼–½ tsp. red pepper flakes

1. Add all of the ingredients, in the order listed, to the inner pot of the Instant Pot.

2. Lock the lid in place, set the vent to sealing, and press Manual, and cook at high pressure for 4 minutes.

3. Release the pressure manually as soon as cooking time is finished.

Chicken Cheddar Broccoli Soup

Maria Shevlin, Sicklerville, NJ

Makes 4–6 servings

Prep. Time: 15 minutes ⚜ *Cooking Time: 15 minutes*

1 lb. chicken breast, thinly chopped/sliced

1 lb. fresh broccoli, chopped

½ cup chopped onion

2 cloves garlic, minced

1 cup shredded carrots

½ cup finely chopped celery

¼ cup finely chopped red bell pepper

3 cups low-sodium chicken bone broth

½ tsp. salt

¼ tsp. black pepper

½ tsp. garlic powder

1 tsp. parsley flakes

Pinch red pepper flakes

2 cups evaporated skim milk

8 oz. freshly shredded cheddar cheese

2 Tbsp. Frank's RedHot® Original Cayenne Pepper Sauce

1. Place chicken, broccoli, chopped onion, garlic, carrots, celery, bell pepper, chicken broth, and seasonings in the pot and stir to mix.

2. Secure the lid and make sure vent is at sealing. Manually set the cook time for 15 minutes on high pressure.

3. Manually release the pressure when cook time is up. Remove the lid, and stir in evaporated milk.

4. Place pot on sauté setting until it all comes to a low boil, approximately 5 minutes.

5. Stir in cheese and the hot sauce.

6. Turn off the pot by pressing Cancel as soon as you add the cheese and give it a stir.

7. Continue to stir till the cheese is melted.

Serving suggestion:

Serve it up with slice or two of whole grain bread.

White Chicken Chili

Judy Gascho, Woodburn, OR

Makes 6 servings
Prep. Time: 20 minutes ⚜ Cooking Time: 30 minutes

2 Tbsp. cooking oil

1½–2 lb. boneless chicken breasts or thighs

1 medium onion, chopped

3 cloves garlic, minced

2 cups chicken broth

3 (15-oz.) cans great northern beans, undrained

15-oz. can white corn, drained

4½-oz. can chopped green chilies, undrained

1 tsp. cumin

½ tsp. ground oregano

1 cup sour cream

1½ cups shredded cheddar or Mexican blend cheese

1. Set Instant Pot to Sauté and allow the inner pot to get hot.

2. Add oil and chicken. Brown chicken on both sides.

3. Add onion, garlic, chicken broth, undrained beans, drained corn, undrained green chilies, cumin, and oregano.

4. Secure the lid and set the valve to sealing.

5. Set to Bean/Chili for 30 minutes.

6. Let pressure release naturally for 15 minutes before manually releasing any remaining pressure.

7. Remove chicken and shred.

8. Put chicken, sour cream, and cheese in the inner pot. Stir until cheese is melted.

Serving suggestion:
Can serve with chopped cilantro and additional cheese.

The Best Bean and Ham Soup

Hope Comerford, Clinton Township, MI

Makes 8–10 servings
Prep. Time: 10 minutes   Soaking Time: 12–24 hours   Cooking Time: 40 minutes

1 Tbsp. olive oil

1 cup chopped onions

2 cloves garlic, minced

1 cup chopped celery

8–10 cups water, *divided*

1 meaty ham bone or shank

1 lb. dry navy beans, soaked overnight, rinsed

¼ cup chopped parsley

1 Tbsp. salt

1 tsp. pepper

1 tsp. nutmeg

1 tsp. oregano

1 tsp. basil

1 bay leaf

1 cup mashed potato flakes

1. Set the Instant Pot to Sauté and add in the olive oil to heat.

2. Sauté the onions, garlic, and celery for 5 minutes.

3. Pour in 1 cup of water and scrape any bit off the bottom of the Inner Pot. Press Cancel.

4. Place the ham bone in inner pot, then pour in all the remaining ingredients except mashed potato flakes.

5. Fill with the remaining water, or until ⅔ of the way full.

6. Secure the lid and set the vent to sealing. Manually set the cook time for 35 minutes on high pressure.

7. When cook time is up, let the pressure release naturally.

8. When the pin drops, carefully remove the lid and stir in the mashed potato flakes. Remove bay leaf. Let the soup thicken for a few minutes, then serve.

Potato Bacon Soup

Colleen Heatwole, Burton, MI

Makes 4–6 servings
Prep. Time: 30 minutes & Cooking Time: 5 minutes

5 lb. potatoes, peeled and cubed

3 stalks of celery, diced into roughly ¼-
to ½-inch pieces

1 large onion, chopped

1 clove garlic, minced

1 Tbsp. seasoning salt

½ tsp. black pepper

4 cups chicken broth

1 lb. bacon, fried crisp and rough
chopped

1 cup half-and-half

1 cup milk, 2% or whole

sour cream, shredded cheddar cheese,
and diced green onion to garnish,
optional

1. Place potatoes in bottom of the Instant Pot inner pot.

2. Add celery, onion, garlic, seasoning salt, and pepper, then stir to combine.

3. Add chicken broth and bacon to pot and stir to combine.

4. Secure the lid and make sure vent is in the sealing position. Manually set the cook time for 5 minutes on high pressure.

5. Manually release the pressure when cooking time is up. Open pot and roughly mash potatoes, leaving some large chunks if desired.

6. Add half-and-half and milk slowly and stir.

7. Serve while still hot with desired assortment of garnishes.

Split Pea Soup

Judy Gascho, Woodburn, OR

Makes 3–4 servings
Prep. Time: 20 minutes   ♨   Cooking Time: 15 minutes

4 cups chicken broth

4 sprigs thyme

4 oz. ham, diced (about ⅓ cup)

2 Tbsp. butter

2 stalks celery

2 carrots

1 large leek

3 cloves garlic

1 cup dried green split peas (about 12 oz.)

Salt to taste

Pepper to taste

1. Pour the broth into the inner pot of the Instant Pot and set to Sauté. Add the thyme, ham, and butter.

2. While the broth heats, chop the celery and cut the carrots into ½-inch-thick rounds. Halve the leek lengthwise and thinly slice and chop the garlic. Add the vegetables to the pot as you cut them. Rinse the split peas in a colander, discarding any stones, then add to the pot.

3. Secure the lid, making sure the steam valve is in the sealing position. Set the cooker to Manual at high pressure for 15 minutes. When the time is up, carefully turn the steam valve to the venting position to release the pressure manually.

4. Turn off the Instant Pot. Remove the lid and stir the soup; discard the thyme sprigs.

5. Thin the soup with up to 1 cup of water if needed (the soup will continue to thicken as it cools). Season with salt and pepper.

Spicy Black Bean Sweet Potato Stew

Maria Shevlin, Sicklerville, NJ

Makes 3–4 servings
Prep. Time: 5 minutes & Cooking Time: 10 minutes

2 tsp. olive oil

4 cloves garlic, minced

1 large onion, diced

8-oz. package mushrooms, chopped

1¾ cups water

2 (14½-oz.) cans petite diced tomatoes

15½-oz. can black beans, drained and rinsed

4 sweet potatoes, peeled and cubed

1 vegetable bouillon cube

1 Tbsp. garlic powder

1 Tbsp. onion powder

1 Tbsp. parsley flakes

2 tsp. paprika

1 tsp. cumin

3 heaping Tbsp. Emeril's® Essence Original Seasoning Blend, *optional*

1. Set the Instant Pot to Sauté, then add the olive oil, garlic, and onion. Cook until just translucent.

2. Add the mushrooms and cook for 2 minutes longer.

3. Pour in the water and scrape up any bits from the bottom of the inner pot.

4. Add the remaining ingredients and stir.

5. Secure the lid and set the vent to sealing. Manually set the cook time for 8 minutes on high pressure.

6. When cook time is up, let the pressure release naturally for 5 minutes then manually release the remaining pressure.

Note:

If you don't want it spicy, you can omit the essence

Serving suggestion:

Serve with steamed rice, green onion, sour cream, or shredded sharp cheese.

Veggie Minestrone

Dorothy VanDeest, Memphis, TN

Makes 8 servings

Prep. Time: 5 minutes ❧ Cooking Time: 4 minutes

2 Tbsp. olive oil

I large onion, chopped

I clove garlic, minced

4 cups chicken or vegetable stock

16-oz. can kidney beans, rinsed and drained

14½-oz. can diced tomatoes

2 medium carrots, sliced thin

¼ tsp. dried oregano

¼ tsp. pepper

½ cup whole wheat elbow macaroni, uncooked

4 oz. fresh spinach

½ cup grated Parmesan cheese

1. Set the Instant Pot to the Sauté function and heat the olive oil.

2. When the olive oil is heated, add the onion and garlic to the inner pot and sauté for 5 minutes.

3. Press Cancel and add the stock, kidney beans, diced tomatoes, carrots, oregano, and pepper. Gently pour in the macaroni, but *do not stir*. Just push the noodles gently under the liquid.

4. Secure the lid and set the vent to sealing.

5. Manually set the cook time for 4 minutes on high pressure.

6. When the cook time is over, manually release the pressure and remove the lid when the pin drops.

7. Stir in the spinach and let wilt a few minutes.

8. Sprinkle 1 Tbsp. grated Parmesan on each individual bowl of the soup. Enjoy!

Flavorful Tomato Soup

Shari Ladd, Hudson, MI

Makes 4 servings

Prep. Time: 10 minutes ☙ Cooking Time: 5 minutes

1 Tbsp. extra-virgin olive oil

2 Tbsp. chopped onion

1 qt. stewed tomatoes

2 tsp. turbinado sugar

½ tsp. pepper

¼ tsp. dried basil

½ tsp. dried oregano

¼ tsp. dried thyme

6 Tbsp. margarine

3 Tbsp. flour

2 cups skim milk

1. Set the Instant Pot to Sauté and heat the olive oil.

2. Sauté the onion for 5 minutes in the heated oil in the inner pot.

3. Press Cancel and add the tomatoes, sugar, pepper, basil, oregano, and thyme.

4. Secure the lid and set the vent to sealing.

5. Manually set the cook time for 5 minutes on high pressure.

6. When the cooking time is over, let the pressure release naturally for 15 minutes, then manually release the remaining pressure.

7. While the pressure is releasing, in a small pot on the stove, melt the margarine. Once the margarine is melted, whisk in the flour and cook for 2 minutes, whisking constantly.

8. Slowly whisk the skim milk into the pot.

9. When the pin has dropped next to the pressure valve, remove the lid and slowly whisk the milk/margarine/flour mixture into the tomato soup.

10. Use an immersion blender to puree the soup. Serve and enjoy!

Main Dishes

Beef

Pot Roast

Carole Whaling, New Tripoli, PA

Makes 8 servings
Prep. Time: 20 minutes ❧ Cooking Time: 35 minutes

2 Tbsp. olive oil

3–4-lb. rump roast, or pot roast, bone removed, and cut into serving-sized pieces, trimmed of fat

4 medium potatoes, cubed or sliced

4 medium carrots, sliced

1 medium onion, sliced

1 tsp. salt

½ tsp. pepper

1 cup beef broth

1. Press the Sauté button on the Instant Pot and add the olive oil. Once the oil is heated, lightly brown the pieces of roast, about 2 minutes on each side. Press Cancel.

2. Place the vegetables into the Instant Pot along with the salt, pepper, and beef broth.

3. Secure the lid and make sure the vent is set to sealing. Manually set the cook time for 35 minutes on high pressure.

4. When cook time is up, let the pressure release naturally.

Pot Roast with Tomato Sauce

Carol Eveleth, Cheyenne, WY

Makes 4–6 servings
Prep. Time: 20 minutes ⚜ Cooking Time: 2 hours

2 lb. beef roast, boneless

¼ tsp. salt

¼ tsp. pepper

1 Tbsp. olive oil

2 stalks celery, chopped

4 Tbsp. margarine

2 cups low-sodium tomato juice

2 cloves garlic, finely chopped, or 1 tsp. garlic powder

1 tsp. thyme

1 bay leaf

4 carrots, chopped

1 medium onion, chopped

4 medium potatoes, chopped

1. Pat beef dry with paper towels; season on all sides with salt and pepper.

2. Select Sauté function on the Instant Pot and adjust heat to More. Put the oil in the inner pot, then cook the beef in oil for 6 minutes, until browned, turning once. Set on plate.

3. Add celery and margarine to the inner pot; cook 2 minutes. Stir in tomato juice, garlic, thyme, and bay leaf. Hit Cancel to turn off Sauté function.

4. Place beef on top of the contents of the inner pot and press into sauce. Cover and lock lid and make sure vent is at sealing. Manually set the cook time at high pressure for 1 hour 15 minutes.

5. Once cooking is complete, let the pressure release naturally. Transfer beef to cutting board. Discard bay leaf.

6. Skim off any excess fat from surface. Choose Sauté function and adjust heat to More. Cook 18 minutes, or until reduced by about half (2½ cups). Hit Cancel to turn off Sauté function.

7. Add carrots, onion, and potatoes. Cover and lock lid and make sure vent is at sealing. Manually set the cook time at high pressure for 10 minutes.

8. Once cooking is complete, manually release the pressure. Using Sauté function, keep at a simmer.

9. Season with more salt and pepper to taste.

Hot Beef Sandwiches

Hope Comerford, Clinton Township, MI

Makes 12 servings
Prep. Time: 5 minutes   &   Cooking Time: 60 minutes

3-lb. rump roast
2 cups beef broth
2 (0.87-oz.) pkgs. beef gravy mix
1 tsp. garlic powder
1 tsp. onion powder
¼ tsp. pepper
6–8 slices of bread

1. Place the roast into the inner pot of the Instant Pot.

2. Mix together the beef broth with beef gravy mix, garlic powder, onion powder, and pepper. Pour it over the roast.

3. Secure the lid and set the vent to sealing. Manually set the cook time for 60 minutes on high pressure.

4. When the cook time is over, let the pressure release naturally.

5. When the pin drops, remove the lid. Remove the beef to a bowl and shred it between 2 forks. Stir it back through the sauce in the inner pot.

6. Serve over slices of bread.

Steak Stroganoff

Hope Comerford, Clinton Township, MI

Makes 6 servings
Prep. Time: 35 minutes   Cooking Time: 20 minutes

3–4 Tbsp. olive oil

½ cup flour

½ tsp. garlic powder

½ tsp. onion powder

½ tsp. salt

⅛ tsp. pepper

2-lb. boneless beef chuck roast, trimmed of fat, cut into 1½ × ½-inch strips

9 oz. sliced mushrooms

½ cup chopped red onion

1 cup beef stock

10¾-oz. can condensed cream of mushroom soup

⅓ cup liquid aminos or soy sauce

½ cup fat-free sour cream

6 servings of cooked egg noodles, elbow noodles, or brown rice ramen noodles

1. Place the oil in the Instant Pot and press Sauté.

2. Combine the flour, garlic powder, onion powder, salt, and pepper in a medium bowl. Stir the beef pieces through the flour mixture until they are evenly coated.

3. Lightly brown the steak pieces in the oil in the Instant Pot, about 2 minutes each side. Let them drain and cool on a paper towel. Do this in batches, adding more oil to the pot with each batch if needed. Set them aside.

4. Pour the mushrooms and red onion into the inner pot and sauté for about 5 minutes.

5. Pour the stock into the inner pot and scrape the bottom vigorously. This will prevent you from getting a burn notice when the Instant Pot pressurizes.

6. Stir in the cream of mushroom soup and liquid aminos.

7. Secure the lid and set the vent to sealing. Manually set the cook time for 10 minutes on high pressure.

8. When the cook time is over, let the pressure release naturally for 10 minutes, then release the rest manually.

9. Remove the lid and switch the Instant Pot to the Sauté function. Stir in the sour cream. Let the sauce come to a boil and cook for about 5 minutes.

10. Serve over the cooked noodles.

Garlic Beef Stroganoff

Sharon Miller, Holmesville, OH

Makes 6 servings
Prep. Time: 20 minutes ⚜ *Cooking Time: 15 minutes*

2 Tbsp. canola oil

1½ lb. boneless round steak, cut into thin strips, trimmed of fat

2 tsp. sodium-free beef bouillon powder

1 cup mushroom juice, with water added to make a full cup

2 (4½-oz.) jars sliced mushrooms, drained, with juice reserved

10¾-oz. can cream of mushroom soup

1 large onion, chopped

3 cloves garlic, minced

1 Tbsp. Worcestershire sauce

6 oz. cream cheese, cubed and softened

1. Press the Sauté button and put the oil into the Instant Pot inner pot.

2. Once the oil is heated, sauté the steak until it is lightly browned, about 2 minutes on each side. Set the beef aside for a moment. Press Cancel and wipe out the Instant Pot with some paper towels.

3. Press Sauté again and dissolve the bouillon in the mushroom juice and water in inner pot of the Instant Pot. Once dissolved, press Cancel.

4. Add the mushrooms, soup, onion, garlic, and Worcestershire sauce and stir. Add the steak back to the pot.

5. Secure the lid and make sure the vent is set to sealing. Press Manual and set for 15 minutes.

6. When cook time is up, let the pressure release naturally for 15 minutes, then perform a Manual release.

7. Press Cancel and remove the lid. Press Sauté. Stir in cream cheese until smooth.

8. Serve over noodles.

Philly Cheese Steaks

Michele Ruvola, Vestal, NY

Makes 6 servings
Prep. Time: 15 minutes ❧ Cooking Time: 11 minutes

1 red pepper, sliced
1 green pepper, sliced
1 onion, sliced
2 cloves garlic, minced
2½ lb. thinly sliced steak
1 tsp. salt
½ tsp. black pepper
0.7-oz. pkg. dry Italian dressing mix
1 cup water
1 beef bouillon cube
6 slices provolone cheese
6 hoagie rolls

1. Put all ingredients in the inner pot of the Instant Pot, except the provolone cheese and rolls.

2. Seal the lid, make sure vent is at sealing. Manually set the cook for 6 minutes on high pressure.

3. When cook time is up, let the pressure release naturally for 10 minutes, then manually release the remaining pressure.

4. Scoop meat and vegetables into rolls.

5. Top with provolone cheese and put on a baking sheet.

6. Broil in oven for 5 minutes.

7. Pour remaining juice in pot into cups for dipping.

Zesty Swiss Steak

Marilyn Mowry, Irving, TX

Makes 6 servings
Prep. Time: 35 minutes ⚜ *Cooking Time: 35 minutes*

3–4 Tbsp. flour
½ tsp. salt
¼ tsp. pepper
1½ tsp. dry mustard
1½–2 lb. round steak, trimmed of fat
1 Tbsp. canola oil
1 cup sliced onions
1 lb. carrots, sliced
14½-oz. can whole tomatoes
⅓ cup water
1 Tbsp. brown sugar
1½ Tbsp. Worcestershire sauce

1. Combine flour, salt, pepper, and dry mustard.

2. Cut steak into serving pieces. Dredge in flour mixture.

3. Set the Instant Pot to Sauté and add in the oil. Brown the steak pieces on both sides in the oil. Press Cancel.

4. Add onions and carrots into the Instant Pot.

5. Combine the tomatoes, water, brown sugar, and Worcestershire sauce. Pour into the Instant Pot.

6. Secure the lid and make sure the vent is set to sealing. Manually set the cook time for 35 minutes on high pressure.

7. When cook time is up, let the pressure release naturally for 15 minutes, then manually release the remaining pressure.

Meatloaf

Hope Comerford, Clinton Township, MI

Makes 6–8 servings

Prep. Time: 10 minutes ⚬ Cooking Time: 25 minutes ⚬ Standing Time: 10 minutes

Nonstick cooking spray

2 lb. ground beef

2 eggs

⅔ cup panko bread crumbs

½ envelope of dry onion soup mix

1 tsp. garlic powder

1 tsp. salt

½ tsp. pepper

1 cup water

1. Mix all ingredients listed except the water in a bowl.

2. Pour the cup of water into the inner pot of the Instant Pot and place the trivet with handles on top.

3. Spray the inside of a 7-inch baking pan with nonstick spray. Press the meatloaf mixture into the baking pan. Cover the pan with aluminum foil.

4. Place the pan on top of the trivet. Secure the lid and set the vent to sealing.

5. Manually set the cook time for 25 minutes on high pressure.

6. When cook time is up, manually release the pressure.

7. When the pin drops, carefully remove the lid and trivet. Let the meatloaf cool for about 10 minutes before slicing.

Serving suggestion:

Drizzle with ketchup before serving.

Lasagna the Instant Pot Way

Hope Comerford, Clinton Township, MI

Makes 8 servings
Prep. Time: 15 minutes & Cooking Time: 7 minutes

1 Tbsp. olive oil
1 lb. extra-lean ground beef or ground turkey
½ cup chopped onion
½ tsp. salt
⅛ tsp. pepper
2 cups water
12 lasagna noodles
8 oz. cottage cheese
1 egg
1 tsp. Italian seasoning
4 cups spinach, chopped or torn
1 cup sliced mushrooms
28 oz. marinara sauce
1 cup mozzarella cheese

1. Set the Instant Pot to the Sauté function and heat the olive oil. Brown the beef and onion with the salt and pepper. This will take about 5 minutes. Because you're using extra-lean ground beef, there should not be much grease, but if so, you'll need to drain it before continuing. Remove half of the ground beef and set aside. Press Cancel.

2. Pour in the water.

3. Break 4 noodles in half and arrange them on top of the beef and water.

4. Mix together the cottage cheese, egg, and Italian seasoning until the mixture is smooth. Smooth half of this mixture over the lasagna noodles.

5. Layer half of the spinach and half of the mushrooms on top.

6. Break 4 more noodles in half and lay them on top of what you just did. Spread out the remaining cottage cheese mixture.

7. Layer on the remaining spinach and mushrooms, then pour half of the marinara sauce over the top.

8. Finish with breaking the remaining 4 noodles in half and laying them on top of the previous layer. Spread the remaining marinara sauce on top.

9. Secure the lid and set the vent to sealing. Manually set the cook time for 7 minutes on high pressure.

10. When the cook time is over, let the pressure release naturally for 10 minutes, then manually release the remaining pressure.

11. When the pin drops, remove the lid and sprinkle the mozzarella cheese on top. Re-cover for 5 minutes.

12. When the 5 minutes is up, remove the lid. You can let this sit for a while to thicken up on Keep Warm.

Spaghetti and Meatballs

Hope Comerford, Clinton Township, MI

Makes 6 servings
Prep. Time: 5 minutes 🎗 Cooking Time: 10 minutes

1 lb. frozen meatballs

8 oz. uncooked spaghetti pasta

14½-oz. can diced tomatoes with basil, garlic, and oregano

3 cups water

24 oz. of your favorite pasta sauce

1. Pour the meatballs into the inner pot and spread around evenly.

2. Break the pasta in half and place over meatballs in a random pattern to help keep them from clumping all together.

3. Pour the diced tomatoes over the top of the pasta.

4. Pour in the water.

5. Pour in the pasta sauce evenly over the top. Make sure the pasta is completely submerged and push any under that may not yet be covered. DO NOT STIR.

6. Secure the lid and set the vent to sealing.

7. Manually set the cook time for 10 minutes on high pressure.

8. When cook time is up, manually release the pressure.

9. When the pin drops, remove the lid and stir.

Serving suggestion:
Serve with grated Parmesan cheese.

Stuffed Cabbage

Hope Comerford, Clinton Township, MI

Makes 12–15 stuffed cabbage rolls
Prep. Time: 30 minutes   Cooking Time: 20 minutes

12 cups water

1 large head cabbage (you will use about 12–15 leaves)

1 lb. 95%-fat-free ground beef

1 medium onion, chopped

2 cloves garlic, chopped

1 tsp. chopped fresh parsley

¼ tsp. salt

½ tsp. pepper

1 egg, beaten

¾ cup brown rice, uncooked

1 cup water

1 Tbsp. vinegar

16 oz. marinara sauce, *divided*

2 tsp. Italian seasoning

1. Pour the water into the inner pot and press Sauté on the Instant Pot. Bring the water to a boil.

2. Gently lower the cabbage into the water and cook for about 5 minutes, turning to be sure all the outer leaves are softened. Press Cancel.

3. Remove the cabbage and carefully drain the water. Peel off 12 to 15 leaves.

4. In a bowl, mix the beef, onion, garlic, parsley, salt, pepper, egg, and brown rice with a wooden spoon or clean hands.

5. On a clean surface, lay out the cabbage leaves. (You may need to thin some of the thicker ribs of the cabbage leaves with a paring knife.) Evenly divide the filling among the leaves. Roll them burrito style, tucking in the ends and rolling tightly. If you need to, you can use a toothpick to hold them closed.

6. Pour the water and vinegar into the inner pot. Gently place the cabbage rolls into the pot, pouring a little sauce on top of each layer and finishing with a layer of sauce. Sprinkle with the Italian seasoning.

7. Secure the lid and set the vent to sealing.

8. Set the Instant Pot to cook manually for 20 minutes on high pressure.

9. When the cook time is over, let the pressure release naturally for 20 minutes and then manually release the remaining pressure.

10. When the pin drops, remove the lid. Serve hot.

Beef Goulash

Colleen Heatwole, Burton, MI

Makes 6 servings
Prep. Time: 15 minutes   Cooking Time: 50 minutes

2 lb. beef stew meat cut into 2-inch pieces

1 large onion, chopped

3 carrots, cut into 2-inch chunks

1 medium red bell pepper, chopped

1 cup beef broth

¼ cup ketchup

2 tsp. Worcestershire sauce

2 tsp. paprika

2 tsp. minced garlic

1 tsp. salt

1. Place all the ingredients into the inner pot of the Instant Pot.

2. Secure the lid and set the vent to sealing. Manually set the cook time for 50 minutes on high pressure.

3. When the cook time is over, let the pressure release naturally for 20 minutes, then manually release the remaining pressure.

Serving suggestion:

Mashed potatoes and green beans go well as sides, or serve with cooked barley or rice.

Walking Tacos

Hope Comerford, Clinton Township, MI

Makes 10–16 servings
Prep. Time: 10 minutes   Cooking Time: 15 minutes

2 lb. ground beef

2 tsp. garlic powder

2 tsp. onion powder

2 Tbsp. chili powder

1 Tbsp. cumin

1 Tbsp. onion powder

1 Tbsp. garlic powder

1 tsp. salt

½ tsp. oregano

½ tsp. red pepper flakes

1 cup water

10–16 individual-sized bags of Doritos

Suggested toppings:

diced tomatoes, shredded cheese, diced cucumbers, chopped onion, shredded lettuce, sour cream, salsa

1. Place the ground beef into the inner pot of the Instant Pot.

2. In a bowl, mix all of the spices. Sprinkle over the beef. Pour the water around the beef.

3. Secure the lid and set the vent to sealing.

5. Manually set the cook time for 15 minutes on high pressure.

6. When cook time is up, manually release the pressure.

7. When the pin drops, remove the lid and break up the beef with a spoon.

8. To serve, open up the bag of Doritos, crumble the chips in the bag with your hand, add some of the ground beef to the bag, then any additional toppings you desire. Serve each bag with a fork.

Chicken

Rotisserie Chicken

Hope Comerford, Clinton Township, MI

Makes 4 servings
Prep. Time: 5 minutes ☙ Cooking Time: 33 minutes

3-lb. whole chicken

2 Tbsp. olive oil, *divided*

Salt to taste

Pepper to taste

20–30 cloves fresh garlic, peeled and left whole

1 cup chicken stock, broth, or water

2 Tbsp. garlic powder

2 tsp. onion powder

½ tsp. basil

½ tsp. cumin

½ tsp. chili powder

1. Rub the chicken with 1 Tbsp. olive oil and sprinkle with salt and pepper.

2. Place the garlic cloves inside the chicken. Use butcher's twine to secure the legs.

3. Press the Sauté button on the Instant Pot, then add the rest of the olive oil to the inner pot.

4. When the pot is hot, place the chicken inside. You are just trying to sear it, so leave it for about 4 minutes on each side.

5. Remove the chicken and set aside. Place the trivet at the bottom of the inner pot and pour in the chicken stock.

6. Mix together the remaining seasonings and rub them all over the entire chicken.

7. Place the chicken back inside the inner pot, breast-side up, on top of the trivet and secure the lid to the sealing position.

8. Manually set the cook time for 25 minutes on high pressure.

9. When cook time is up, allow the pressure to release naturally for 15 minutes, then manually release any remaining pressure.

10. Let the chicken rest for 5–10 minutes before serving.

Chicken and Dumplings

Bonnie Miller, Louisville, OH

Makes 4 servings
Prep. Time: 10 minutes   Cooking Time: 3 minutes

1 Tbsp. olive oil

1 small onion, chopped

2 celery ribs, cut into 1-inch pieces

6 small carrots, cut into 1-inch chunks

2 cups chicken broth

2 lb. boneless, skinless chicken breast halves, cut into 1-inch pieces

2 chicken bouillon cubes

1 tsp. salt

1 tsp. pepper

1 tsp. poultry seasoning

Biscuits:

2 cups buttermilk biscuit mix

½ cup plus 1 Tbsp. milk

1 tsp. parsley

1. Set the Instant Pot to the Sauté function and heat the olive oil.

2. Add the onion, celery, and carrots to the hot oil and sauté for 3 to 5 minutes.

3. Pour in the broth and scrape the bottom of the inner pot with a wooden spoon or spatula to deglaze. Press Cancel.

4. Add the chicken, bouillon, salt, pepper, and poultry seasoning.

5. Combine the biscuit ingredients in a bowl until just moistened. Drop 2-Tbsp. mounds over the contents of the inner pot, as evenly spaced out as possible.

6. Secure the lid and set the vent to sealing. Manually set the cook time for 3 minutes.

7. When the cook time is over, manually release the pressure.

Chicken Dinner in a Packet

Bonnie Whaling, Clearfield, PA

Makes 4 servings
Prep. Time: 10 minutes ❧ Cooking Time: 15 minutes

1 cup water

4 (5-oz.) boneless, skinless chicken breast halves

2 cups sliced fresh mushrooms

2 medium carrots, cut in thin strips, about 1 cup

1 medium zucchini, unpeeled and sliced, about 1½ cups

2 Tbsp. olive oil or canola oil

2 Tbsp. lemon juice

1 Tbsp. fresh basil or 1 tsp. dry basil

¼ tsp. salt

¼ tsp. black pepper

1. Pour the water into the inner pot of the Instant Pot and place the trivet or a steamer basket on top.

2. Fold four 12-inch × 28-inch pieces of foil in half to make four 12-inch × 14-inch rectangles. Place one chicken breast half on each piece of foil.

3. Top with the mushrooms, carrots, and zucchini, dividing the vegetables equally between the chicken bundles.

4. In a small bowl, stir together the oil, lemon juice, basil, salt, and pepper.

5. Drizzle the oil mixture over the vegetables and chicken.

6. Pull up two opposite edges of foil. Seal with a double fold. Then fold in the remaining edges, leaving enough space for steam to build.

7. Place the bundles on top of the trivet, or inside the steamer basket.

8. Secure the lid and set the vent to sealing.

9. Manually set the cook time for 15 minutes at high pressure.

10. When the cooking time is over, let the pressure release naturally. When the pin drops, remove the lid.

11. Serve dinners in foil packets, or transfer to serving plate.

Lime-Like Key West Chicken

Maria Shevlin, Sicklerville, NJ

Makes 4 servings
Prep. Time: 5 minutes ☙ *Cooking Time: 12 minutes*

1 Tbsp. avocado oil

2 cloves garlic, minced

2½ lb. boneless skinless chicken breasts

½ tsp. garlic powder

½ tsp salt

¼ tsp white pepper

1 Tbsp. parsley flakes

¼ cup chicken stock

¼ cup coconut aminos or tamari

Juice of 1 lime

Zest from one lime

2 Tbsp. honey

2 Tbsp. brown sugar or brown sugar substitute

1. Set the Instant Pot to the Sauté function. Add the avocado oil and garlic to the inner pot and sauté for 2 minutes. Press Cancel.

2. Add the chicken, garlic powder, salt, white pepper, and parsley flakes to the inner pot. Mix well to coat.

3. In a small bowl combine the chicken stock, coconut aminos, lime juice, zest, honey, and brown sugar.

4. Pour over the chicken.

5. Secure the lid and set the vent to sealing.

6. Manually set the cook time for 12 minutes on high pressure.

7. When cook time is up, let the pressure release naturally for 10 minutes, the manually release any remaining pressure.

8. Optional: Remove and shred the chicken with a hand mixer, then return it back to the pot and stir it into the juices.

Serving suggestion:
Serve as tacos if using shredded.

Crustless Chicken Potpie

Hope Comerford, Clinton Township, MI

Makes 6 servings
Prep. Time: 15 minutes ♣ Cooking Time: 30 minutes

1 lb. boneless, skinless chicken breasts

3 Yukon Gold potatoes, peeled and chopped into ½-inch cubes

1 cup chopped onion

2 carrots, chopped

¾ cup frozen peas

¾ cup frozen corn

½ cup chopped celery

10¾-oz. can condensed cream of chicken soup

1 cup milk

1 cup chicken broth

1 tsp. salt

1 tsp. garlic powder

1 tsp. onion powder

2 Tbsp. cornstarch

2 Tbsp. cold water

16.3-oz. can flaky biscuits

1. Place all the ingredients, except for the cornstarch, water, and biscuits, into the inner pot of the Instant Pot.

2. Secure the lid and set the vent to sealing. Manually set the cook time for 25 minutes on high pressure.

3. While the Instant Pot is cooking, bake the canned biscuits according to the directions on the can.

4. When the cook time is over, manually release the pressure.

5. When the pin drops, remove the lid. Remove the chicken to a bowl. Press Cancel then press Sauté.

6. Mix together the cornstarch and water. Stir this into the contents of the Instant Pot and cook until thickened, about 5 minutes. Meanwhile, shred the chicken, then add it back in with the contents of the inner pot.

7. Serve with the freshly baked flaky biscuits.

Chicken in Mushroom Gravy

Rosemarie Fitzgerald, Gibsonia, PA
Audrey L. Kneer, Williamsfield, IL

Makes 6 servings
Prep. Time: 5 minutes ⚘ Cooking Time: 10 minutes

6 (5 oz. each) boneless, skinless chicken breast halves

Salt and pepper to taste

¼ cup dry white wine

¼ cup chicken broth

10¾-oz. can cream of mushroom soup

4 oz. sliced mushrooms

1. Place chicken in the inner pot of the Instant Pot. Season with salt and pepper.

2. Combine wine, broth, and soup in a bowl, then pour over the chicken. Top with the mushrooms.

3. Secure the lid and make sure the vent is set to sealing. Set on Manual mode for 10 minutes.

4. When cooking time is up, let the pressure release naturally.

Chicken and Noodles

Hope Comerford, Clinton Township, MI

Makes 4 servings
Prep. Time: 8 minutes   Cooking Time: 13 minutes

1 Tbsp. olive oil

½ cup chopped onion

3 cloves garlic, minced

1 cup diced carrots

⅓ cup diced celery

3 lb. boneless skinless chicken breasts, cut into ½-inch pieces

2½ cups low-sodium chicken stock

1 tsp. sea salt

½ tsp. Italian seasoning

¼ tsp. pepper

4 cups egg noodles

¾ cup cream

2 Tbsp. cornstarch

¼ cup chopped fresh parsley

1. Set the Instant Pot to the Sauté function and heat the olive oil.

2. Sauté the onion and garlic for 2 minutes in the oil.

3. Add the carrots and celery to the inner pot and sauté for about 3 additional minutes.

4. Add the chicken pieces and sauté for an additional 3 minutes.

5. Pour in the chicken stock and deglaze the bottom of the inner pot by scraping up any bits. Press Cancel.

6. Stir in the salt and Italian seasoning. Pour in the egg noodles and push under the liquid.

7. Secure the lid and set the vent to sealing.

8. Manually set the cook time for 2 minutes.

9. When cook time is up, let the pressure release naturally for 5 minutes, then manually release the remaining pressure. Press Cancel.

10. When the pin drops, carefully remove the lid.

11. In a small bowl, whisk together the cream and cornstarch.

12. Set the Instant Pot to Sauté and slowly stir in the cream and cornstarch mixture.

13. Let the mixture simmer for about 3 minutes, or until thickened.

14. Garnish with the fresh parsley.

Skinny Chicken Stroganoff

Carol Sherwood, Batavia, NY

Makes 6 servings
Prep. Time: 10 minutes ⚶ Cooking Time: 5 minutes

1 tsp. olive oil

1 cup chopped onion

1 clove garlic, pressed

1½ lb. boneless, skinless chicken breasts, cut into bite-sized pieces

⅛ tsp. black pepper

8 oz. uncooked whole wheat wide egg noodles

8 oz. sliced fresh mushrooms

1 cup chicken broth

¾ cup sour cream

4 slices turkey bacon, cooked and broken, *optional*

2 Tbsp. chopped fresh parsley, *optional*

2 Tbsp. cornstarch

2 Tbsp. cold water

1. Set the Instant Pot to Sauté and heat the olive oil in the inner pot.

2. Sauté the onion and garlic for 3 minutes. Press Cancel.

3. Add the chicken and pepper. Stir to coat everything in the pot. Pour the noodles on top of the chicken mixture. Evenly spread out. Evenly spread the mushrooms on top of the noodles.

4. Pour the chicken broth on top. Secure the lid and set the vent to sealing.

5. Manually set the cook time for 2 minutes at high pressure.

6. When the cooking time is over, let the pressure release naturally for 10 minutes, then manually release the remaining pressure.

7. When the pin drops, remove the lid. Stir.

8. Remove about ¼ cup of the liquid from the inner pot, and, in a separate bowl, mix this with the sour cream, tempering it. Slowly add this tempered sour cream to the inner pot, stirring constantly. Stir in the bacon and parsley, if desired.

9. Set the Instant Pot to Sauté. In a small bowl, whisk together the cornstarch and water. Add this to the inner pot and stir. Cook for a couple of minutes, or until thickened to your liking, then press Cancel.

Insta Pasta à la Maria

Maria Shevlin, Sicklerville, MI

Makes 6–8 servings
Prep. Time: 10–15 minutes ⚲ *Cooking Time: 6 minutes*

32-oz. jar of your favorite spaghetti sauce or 1 qt. of homemade

2 cups fresh chopped spinach

1 cup chopped mushrooms

½ precooked whole rotisserie chicken, shredded

1 tsp. salt

½ tsp. black pepper

½ tsp. dried basil

¼ tsp. red pepper flakes

1 tsp. parsley flakes

13¼-oz. box pasta, any shape or brand

3 cups water

1. Place the sauce in the bottom of the inner pot of the Instant Pot.

2. Add in the spinach, then the mushrooms.

3. Add the chicken on top of the veggies and sauce.

4. Add the seasonings and give it a stir to mix.

5. Add the box of pasta.

6. Add 3 cups of water.

7. Secure the lid and move vent to sealing. Manually set for 6 minutes on high pressure.

8. When cook time is up, release the pressure manually.

9. Remove the lid and stir to mix.

Cheesy Chicken and Rice

Amanda Breeden, Timberville, VA

Makes 5–6 servings
Prep. Time: 5 minutes ⚬ Cooking Time: 30 minutes

3 cups low-sodium chicken broth

2 cups brown rice

1 lb. frozen boneless, skinless chicken breasts

3 cups shredded reduced-fat cheddar cheese

1. Add the chicken broth, rice, and frozen chicken to the inner pot of the Instant Pot.

2. Secure the lid and set the vent to sealing. Cook on high pressure setting for 30 minutes.

3. When done cooking, release the pressure manually and stir everything together.

4. Stir the cheese into the dish until it is melted and blended evenly. Serve and enjoy!

Turkey

Traditional Turkey Breast

Hope Comerford, Clinton Township, MI

Makes 6 servings
Prep. Time: 10 minutes 🝔 Cooking Time: 35 minutes

7-lb. or less turkey breast

2 cups turkey broth

1–2 Tbsp. olive oil

Rub:

2 tsp. garlic powder

1 tsp. onion powder

1 tsp. salt

¼ tsp. pepper

1 tsp. poultry seasoning

1. Remove the gizzards from the turkey breast, rinse it, and pat it dry.

2. Place the trivet into the inner pot of the Instant Pot, then pour in the broth.

3. Mix together the rub ingredients in a small bowl.

4. Rub the turkey all over with olive oil, then press the rub onto the turkey breast all over.

5. Place the turkey breast onto the trivet, breast-side up.

6. Secure the lid and set the vent to sealing. Manually set the cook time for 35 minutes on high pressure.

7. When the cook time is over, let the pressure release naturally.

Tip:

If you want the breast to have crispy skin, remove it from the Instant Pot and place it under the broiler in the oven for a few minutes, or until skin is as crispy as you like it.

Turkey and Mushroom Scallopine à la Mamma Ree

Maria Shevlin, Sicklerville, NJ

Makes 3–4 servings

Prep. Time: 5 minutes ☙ Cooking Time: 20 minutes

2 Tbsp. butter

1 Tbsp. olive oil

3–4 cloves garlic, chopped fine

½ cup white wine or chicken stock

2 tsp. Italian seasoning

½ tsp. black pepper

1 tsp. garlic powder

6 thin cut turkey breasts cutlets, sliced into strips

1 medium onion, cut into thin strips

1 lb. mushrooms, sliced

1. Set the Instant Pot to Sauté, then add the butter, oil, and chopped garlic. Cook approximately 3 minutes.

2. Add the stock or wine, and seasonings. Scrape the bottom of the pot to bring up any stuck-on bits.

3. Add the turkey strips, onion, and mushrooms. Stir.

4. Secure the lid and set the vent to sealing.

5. Manually set the cook time for 20 minutes on high pressure.

6. Let the pressure release naturally for 10 minutes, then manually release the remaining pressure if needed.

Serving suggestion:

Serve over thin egg noodles, or with a side of green beans/haricot verts.

Ground Turkey Cacciatore Spaghetti

Maria Shevlin, Sicklerville, NJ

Makes 6 servings
Prep. Time: 15–20 minutes   ⚬   Cooking Time: 6 minutes

1 tsp. olive oil

1 medium sweet onion, chopped

3 cloves garlic, minced

1 lb. ground turkey

32-oz. jar spaghetti sauce, or 1 qt. homemade

1 tsp. salt

½ tsp. black pepper

½ tsp. oregano

½ tsp. dried basil

½ tsp. red pepper flakes

1 cup bell pepper strips, mixed colors if desired

1 cup diced mushrooms

13¼-oz. box Dreamfields spaghetti

3 cups chicken bone broth

1. Press the Sauté button on the Instant Pot and add the oil, onion, and garlic to the inner pot.

2. Add in the ground turkey and break it up a little while it browns.

3. Once ground turkey is browned, add in the sauce and seasonings.

4. Add in the bell peppers and mushrooms and give it a stir to mix.

5. Add in the spaghetti—break it in half in order to fit it in.

6. Add in the chicken bone broth.

7. Lock lid, make sure the vent is set to sealing, and set on Manual at high pressure for 6 minutes.

8. When cook time is up, manually release the pressure.

Serving suggestion:
Top with some fresh grated Parmesan cheese and basil.

Pizza in a Pot

Marianne J. Troyer, Millersburg, OH

Makes 8 servings

Prep. Time: 25 minutes   Cooking Time: 15 minutes

1 lb. bulk lean sweet Italian turkey sausage, browned and drained

28-oz. can crushed tomatoes

15½-oz. can chili beans

2¼-oz. can sliced black olives, drained

1 medium onion, chopped

1 small green bell pepper, chopped

2 cloves garlic, minced

¼ cup grated Parmesan cheese

1 Tbsp. quick-cooking tapioca

1 Tbsp. dried basil

1 bay leaf

1. Set the Instant Pot to Sauté, then add the turkey sausage. Sauté until browned.

2. Add the remaining ingredients into the Instant Pot and stir.

3. Secure the lid and make sure the vent is set to sealing. Cook on Manual for 15 minutes.

4. When cook time is up, let the pressure release naturally for 5 minutes then manually release any remaining pressure. Discard bay leaf.

Cheesy Stuffed Cabbage

Maria Shevlin, Sicklerville, NJ

Makes 6–8 servings
Prep. Time: 30 minutes & Cooking Time: 18 minutes

1–2 heads savoy cabbage
1 lb. ground turkey
1 egg
1 cup shredded cheddar cheese
2 Tbsp. heavy cream
¼ cup shredded Parmesan cheese
¼ cup shredded mozzarella cheese
¼ cup finely diced onion
¼ cup finely diced bell pepper
¼ cup finely diced mushrooms
1 tsp. salt
½ tsp. black pepper
1 tsp. garlic powder
6 basil leaves, fresh and cut chiffonade
1 Tbsp. fresh parsley, chopped
1 qt. of your favorite pasta sauce

1. Remove the core from the cabbages.

2. Boil water and place 1 head at a time into the water for approximately 10 minutes.

3. Allow cabbage to cool slightly. Once cooled, remove the leaves carefully and set aside. You'll need about 15 or 16.

4. Mix together the meat and all remaining ingredients except the pasta sauce.

5. One leaf at a time, put a heaping Tbsp. of meat mixture in the center.

6. Tuck the sides in and then roll tightly.

7. Add ½ cup sauce to the bottom of the inner pot of the Instant Pot.

8. Place the rolls, fold side down, into the pot and layer them, putting a touch of sauce between each layer and finally on top. (You may want to cook the rolls a half batch at a time.)

9. Lock lid and make sure vent is set to sealing. Set timer on 18 minutes on Manual at high pressure, then manually release the pressure when cook time is over.

Turkey Meatloaf

Delores A. Gnagey, Saginaw, MI

Makes 4–5 servings

Prep. Time: 15 minutes ❧ *Cooking Time: 15 minutes* ❧ *Standing Time: 10 minutes*

1 cup plus 1 Tbsp. water, *divided*

1 lb. lean ground turkey

½ small onion, minced

1½ Tbsp. minced fresh parsley

2 egg whites

2 Tbsp. skim milk

½ tsp. dry mustard

¼ tsp. salt

⅛ tsp. ground white pepper

Pinch nutmeg

1 slice whole wheat bread, lightly toasted, made into coarse crumbs

1 Tbsp. low-sugar ketchup

1. Set the trivet inside the inner pot of the Instant Pot and pour in 1 cup water.

2. In a medium bowl, mix the ground turkey, onion, and parsley. Set aside.

3. In another bowl, whisk the egg whites. Add the milk, mustard, salt, pepper, and nutmeg to the egg. Whisk to blend.

4. Add the breadcrumbs to the egg mixture. Let rest 10 minutes.

5. Add the egg mixture to the meat mixture and blend well.

6. Spray the inside of a 7-inch springform baking pan, then spread the meat mixture into it.

7. Blend together the ketchup and 1 Tbsp. water in a small bowl. Spread the mixture on top of the meat. Cover the pan with aluminum foil.

8. Place the springform pan on top of the trivet inside the inner pot.

9. Secure the lid and set the vent to sealing.

10. Manually set the cook time for 15 minutes on high pressure.

11. When the cooking time is over, let the pressure release naturally.

12. When the pin drops, remove the lid and use oven mitts to carefully remove the trivet from the inner pot.

13. Allow the meat to stand 10 minutes before slicing to serve.

Pork

Paprika Pork Chops with Rice

Sharon Easter, Yuba City, CA

Makes 4 servings
Prep. Time: 5 minutes ❧ Cooking Time: 30 minutes

⅛ tsp. pepper

1 tsp. paprika

1 Tbsp. olive oil

4–5 thick-cut boneless pork chops
(1 inch to 1½ inches thick)

1¼ cups water, *divided*

1 onion, sliced

½ green bell pepper, sliced in rings

1½ cups canned stewed tomatoes

1 cup brown rice

1. Mix the pepper and paprika in a flat dish. Dredge the chops in the seasoning mixture.

2. Set the Instant Pot to the Sauté function and heat the oil in the inner pot.

3. Brown the chops on both sides for 1 to 2 minutes a side. Remove the pork chops and set aside.

4. Pour a small amount of water into the inner pot and scrape up any bits from the bottom with a wooden spoon. Press Cancel.

5. Place the browned chops side by side in the inner pot. Place 1 slice onion and 1 ring of green pepper on top of each chop. Spoon tomatoes with their juices over the top.

6. Pour the rice in and pour the remaining water over the top.

7. Secure the lid and set the vent to sealing.

8. Manually set the cook time for 30 minutes on high pressure.

9. When the cooking time is over, manually release the pressure.

Pork Chops in Mushroom Gravy

Hope Comerford, Clinton Township, MI

Makes 4 servings
Prep. Time: 10 minutes 🍴 Cooking Time: 15 minutes

1 Tbsp. olive oil

2 lb. 1-inch-thick cut bone-in pork chops

½ tsp. sea salt

½ tsp. garlic powder

¼ tsp. pepper

1½ cups beef broth, *divided*

2 cups sliced baby bella mushrooms

1 small onion, sliced into half rings

2 (0.75-oz.) packets of mushroom gravy

2 tsp. Worcestershire sauce

1. Set the Instant Pot to the Sauté function and heat olive oil.

2. Season the pork chops evenly with the salt, garlic powder, and pepper. Brown the pork chops on both sides in the inner pot. Do it in batches if needed. Remove and set aside.

3. Pour in ½ cup of the beef broth and deglaze the bottom of the inner pot. Press Cancel.

4. Place the mushrooms and onion into the pot. Place the pork chops on top.

5. Mix the remaining broth with the mushroom gravy packets and Worcestershire sauce. Pour it over the chops.

6. Secure the lid and set the vent to sealing.

7. Manually set the cook time for 15 minutes on high pressure.

8. When cook time is up, let the pressure release naturally for 10 minutes, then manually release the remaining pressure.

9. Serve and enjoy.

Taylor's Favorite Szechuan Pork

Maria Shevlin, Sicklerville, NJ

Makes 3–4 servings
Prep. Time: 5 minutes ⚬ *Cooking Time: 15 minutes*

2 tsp. olive oil

4 thick boneless loin chops, sliced into thin strips

1 onion, sliced

1 cup water

1-2 heaping Tbsp. chili garlic paste

2 tsp. sugar

3 Tbsp. tomato paste

1 tsp. coconut aminos or soy sauce

2–3 green onions, chopped, *optional*

Sesame seeds, *optional*

1. Set the Instant Pot to Sauté and heat the olive oil.

2. Sauté the pork in the Instant Pot until lightly browned.

3. Toss in the onion; stir until mixed well.

4. Add the water, chili garlic paste, sugar, and tomato paste, and simmer until thickened.

5. Stir in the coconut aminos. Let simmer for 15 minutes.

6. Add as many green onions as you desire and mix well.

7. Top with the optional sesame seeds after plating.

Serving suggestion:

Serve with broccoli with garlic and olive oil, and/or rice or ramen noodles.

BBQ Pork Sandwiches

Carol Eveleth, Cheyenne, WY

Makes 4 servings
Prep. Time: 20 minutes   Cooking Time: 60 minutes

2 tsp. salt

1 tsp. onion powder

1 tsp. garlic powder

1 Tbsp. olive oil

2-lb. pork shoulder roast, cut into 3-inch pieces

2 cups barbecue sauce

1. In a small bowl, combine the salt, onion powder, and garlic powder. Season the pork with the rub.

2. Turn the Instant Pot on to Sauté. Heat the olive oil in the inner pot.

3. Add the pork to the oil and turn to coat. Lock the lid and set vent to sealing.

4. Press Manual and cook on high pressure for 45 minutes.

5. When cooking is complete, release the pressure manually, then open the lid.

6. Using 2 forks, shred the pork, pour barbecue sauce over the pork, then press Sauté. Simmer 3 to 5 minutes. Press Cancel. Toss pork to mix.

Serving suggestion:

Pile the shredded BBQ pork on the bottom half of a bun. Add any additional toppings if you wish, then finish with the top half of the bun.

Pork Baby Back Ribs

Marla Folkerts, Batavia, IL

Maria 6–8 servings
Prep. Time: 20 minutes   *Cooking Time: 30 minutes*

3 racks of ribs
1 cup brown sugar
1 cup white sugar
1 tsp. garlic powder
1 tsp. garlic salt
1 cup water
½ cup apple cider vinegar
1 tsp. liquid smoke
½ cup barbecue sauce

1. Take the membrane/skin off the back of the ribs.

2. Mix together the remaining ingredients (except the barbecue sauce) and slather it on the ribs.

3. Place the ribs around the inside of the inner pot instead of stacking them. Secure the lid in place and make sure vent is at sealing.

4. Use the Meat setting and set for 30 minutes on high pressure.

5. When cooking time is up, let the pressure release naturally for 10 minutes, then do a quick release of the remaining pressure.

6. Place the ribs on a baking sheet and cover them with the barbecue sauce. Broil for 7–10 minutes (watching so they don't burn).

Tip:

I think placing the ribs around the pot instead of stacking makes it easier.

Taylor's Favorite Uniquely Stuffed Peppers

Maria Shevlin, Sicklerville, NJ

Makes 4 servings
Prep. Time: 20–30 minutes ⚜ *Cooking Time: 15 minutes*

4 red bell peppers

I tsp. olive oil

½ onion, chopped

3 cloves garlic, minced

½ lb. ground turkey

½ lb. spicy Italian sausage, sliced

I tsp. salt

½ tsp. black pepper

I tsp. garlic powder

½ tsp. dried oregano

½ tsp. dried basil

I medium zucchini, grated and water pressed out

½ cup of your favorite low-sugar barbecue sauce

¼ cup quick oats

I cup water or low-sodium bone broth

1. Cut the stem part of the top off the bell peppers, remove seeds and membranes, and set aside.

2. Add olive oil, onion, and garlic to a pan. Cook till al dente.

3. Add the ground turkey and sausage, and brown lightly.

4. Add the seasonings, zucchini, and barbecue sauce.

5. Add the oats.

6. Mix well to combine.

7. Stuff the filling inside each pepper—pack it in.

8. Add 1 cup of water or bone broth to the bottom of the inner pot of the Instant Pot.

9. Add the rack to the pot.

10. Arrange the stuffed peppers standing upright.

11. Lock lid, make sure vent is at sealing, and use the Manual setting to set for 15 minutes.

12. When cook time is up, release the pressure manually.

Rice with Beans and Franks

Maria Shevlin, Sicklerville, NJ

Makes 4–6 servings

Prep. Time: 8 minutes ⚜ Cooking Time: 10 minutes

1 tsp. olive oil

1 sweet onion, diced

4–6 slices bacon, uncooked, sliced

¾ cup ketchup

2 Tbsp. yellow mustard (you can also use Dijon for a slight kick)

2 tsp. Worcestershire sauce

1 Tbsp. parsley flakes

1 tsp. garlic powder

1 tsp. onion powder

½–1 tsp. chili powder

¼ tsp. red pepper flakes

3 (15-oz.) cans of your favorite baked beans (we enjoy a variety of Bush's)

8 hot dogs, any type, sliced into rounds

1–2 cups precooked rice, for serving

1. Set the Instant Pot to Sauté and heat up the olive oil. Add the diced onion and bacon. Cook until onions soften and bacon is almost cooked through, not crisp.

2. Add the ketchup, mustard, Worcestershire sauce, parsley, garlic powder, onion powder, chili powder and red pepper flakes. Stir.

3. Add in the beans, then hot dogs. Mix all together one final time.

4. Place the lid on and let it cook for 10 minutes.

5. When the 10 minutes is up, remove the lid and stir in the cooked rice. Press Cancel.

Serving suggestions:

Serve with a side salad and buttered rolls.

Top with green onions or more diced sweet onion.

Meatless

Creamy Mexican Pasta

Maria Shevlin, Sicklerville, NJ

Makes 4–5 servings
Prep. Time: 5 minutes 🖐 Cooking Time: 6 minutes

1 Tbsp. olive oil

½ sweet onion, diced

2 cloves garlic, minced

1 lb. uncooked pasta shells, small or medium-sized

1 Tbsp. taco seasoning

1 tsp. dried cilantro

4 oz. tomato sauce

1 cup mild salsa

1½ cups chicken stock

¼ cup heavy cream

4 oz. softened cream cheese

4 oz. cheddar cheese, shredded

1. Set the Instant Pot to the Sauté function and heat the olive oil.

2. Add the diced onion and garlic and cook for 2 minutes.

3. Press Cancel.

4. Add in the pasta.

5. Add the taco seasoning and cilantro, then tomato sauce, salsa, and stock. Stir well to mix.

6. Secure the lid and set the vent to sealing.

7. Manually set the cook time for 4 minutes on high pressure.

8. When cook time is up, manually release the pressure, then remove the lid when the pin drops.

9. Stir the pasta to ensure its mixed well and coated evenly.

10. Add the heavy cream, cream cheese, and shredded cheese and stir until the cheese has melted.

Serving suggestion:
Top with sour cream and sliced green onions.

Seafood

Seafood & Okra Gumbo

Maria Shevlin, Sicklerville, NJ

Makes 8 servings

Prep. Time: 10 minutes ⚓ Cooking Time: about 28–30 minutes

2 Tbsp. olive oil

1 sweet onion, diced

3 cloves garlic, minced

2 large-sized bell peppers diced (1 red, 1 green)

2 carrots, cut into rings and cut in half

4 oz. mushrooms, sliced

1 cup celery, cut on an angle

3 cups chicken or seafood stock

2 tsp. Cajun seasoning

2 bay leaves

1 tsp. salt

¼ tsp. black pepper

14½-oz. can Ro-Tel® petite diced tomatoes

14½-oz can fire roasted diced tomatoes

1 cup frozen okra

1 lb. shrimp peeled, deveined

2 (10-oz.) cans whole clams

8-oz. pkg chunk imitation crab meat

cooked rice, *optional*

1. Set the Instant Pot to Sauté and heat the oil. Add the onion, garlic, bell peppers, carrots, mushrooms, and celery. Cook for about 3 minutes, stirring constantly.

2. Add the broth or stock, Cajun seasoning, bay leaves, salt, black pepper, and tomatoes.

3. Secure the lid and set the cook time for 20 minutes on high pressure.

4. When cook time is up, manually release the pressure. Press Cancel.

5. When the pin drops remove the lid. Add in the okra, shrimp, and clams. (You can add the clam broth if desired; it will make a slightly thinner gumbo.)

6. Press Sauté and cook for about 4–5 minutes, until the shrimp is cooked.

7. Press Cancel. Stir in the imitation crab once heat is turned off. Remove and discard bay leaves.

8. If desired, you can now add in the cooked rice, or serve it on the side.

Tuna Noodle Casserole

Hope Comerford, Clinton Township, MI

Makes 8 servings
Prep. Time: 10 minutes ⚬ Cooking Time: 2 minutes

4 cups chicken broth

1 tsp. sea salt

1 tsp. garlic powder

1 tsp. onion powder

¼ tsp. pepper

12 oz. egg noodles

2 (5-oz.) cans tuna, drained

2 cups frozen peas and carrots, thawed

½ cup heavy cream

3 cups shredded white cheddar cheese

1. Pour the broth, salt, garlic powder, onion powder, and pepper into the inner pot of the Instant Pot. Stir.

2. Pour in the egg noodles and push under the liquid. Sprinkle the tuna on top.

3. Secure the lid and set the vent to sealing.

4. Manually set the cook time for 2 minutes on high pressure.

5. When cook time is up, let the pressure release naturally.

6. When the pin drops, remove the lid and stir in the peas and carrots.

7. SLOWLY stir in the heavy cream, a little at a time, so it does not curdle.

8. Stir in the shredded cheese, a little at a time. Press Cancel.

9. Let the mixture thicken with the lid off until desired thickness is reached. It will thicken as it cools.

Side Dishes

Macaroni and Cheese

Hope Comerford, Clinton Township, MI

Makes 8 servings
Prep. Time: 5 minutes ⚬ Cooking Time: 4 minutes

1 lb. uncooked elbow macaroni

2 cups water

2 cups chicken broth

4 Tbsp. butter

1 tsp. salt

½ tsp. pepper

1 tsp. hot sauce

1 tsp. dried mustard

½–1 cup heavy cream or milk

1 cup shredded Gouda

1 cup shredded sharp cheddar cheese

1 cup shredded Monterey Jack cheese

1. Place the macaroni, water, broth, butter, salt, pepper, hot sauce, and dried mustard into the inner pot of the Instant Pot.

2. Secure the lid and set the vent to sealing. Manually set the cook time for 4 minutes.

3. When the cook time is over, manually release the pressure.

4. When the pin drops, remove the lid and stir in the cream, starting with ½ cup. Begin stirring in the shredded cheese, 1 cup at a time. If the sauce ends up being too thin, let it sit a while and it will thicken up.

Variation:

If you want the mac and cheese to have a crust on top, pour the mac and cheese from the Instant Pot into an oven-safe baking dish. Top with additional cheese and bake in a 325°F oven for about 15 minutes.

Cheesy Potatoes

Hope Comerford, Clinton Township, MI

Makes 8 servings
Prep. Time: 5 minutes & Cooking Time: 3 minutes

2 Tbsp. butter

1 cup chopped onions

2 cloves garlic, chopped

1 cup chicken broth

30-oz. pkg. frozen hash browns, diced or shredded

1 cup sour cream

1 tsp. sea salt

1 tsp. onion powder

1 tsp. garlic powder

¼ tsp. pepper

2 cups shredded cheddar cheese

1 cup panko breadcrumbs, *optional*

1. Set the Instant Pot to the Sauté function. Add the butter to the inner pot and let it melt.

2. Sauté the onions and garlic in the butter for 3 minutes.

3. Pour in the chicken broth and scrape the bottom of the inner pot with a wooden spoon or spatula. Press Cancel.

4. Place the steamer basket into the inner pot and pour the frozen hash browns into that.

5. Secure the lid and set the vent to sealing. Manually set the cook time for 3 minutes.

6. When the cook time is over, manually release the pressure.

7. When the pin drops, remove the lid, carefully pour the hash browns from the steamer basket into the inner pot, and stir in the sour cream, sea salt, onion powder, garlic powder, pepper, and shredded cheese.

8. If you choose, you can transfer the contents of the inner pot to an oven-safe baking dish. Then top the potatoes with the breadcrumbs and put them under the broiler for 2–3 minutes.

Side Dishes **167**

Bacon Ranch Red Potatoes

Hope Comerford, Clinton Township, MI

Makes 6 servings
Prep. Time: 15 minutes ⚹ *Cooking Time: 7 minutes*

4 strips bacon, chopped into small pieces

2 lb. red potatoes, diced

1 Tbsp. fresh chopped parsley

1 tsp. sea salt

4 cloves garlic, chopped

1-oz. packet ranch dressing/seasoning mix

⅓ cup water

½ cup shredded sharp white cheddar

2 Tbsp. chopped green onions for garnish

1. Set the Instant Pot to Sauté, add the bacon to the inner pot, and cook until crisp.

2. Stir in the potatoes, parsley, sea salt, garlic, ranch dressing/seasoning, and water.

3. Secure the lid, make sure vent is at sealing, then set the Instant Pot to Manual for 7 minutes at high pressure.

4. When cooking time is up, do a quick release and carefully open the lid.

5. Stir in the cheese. Garnish with the green onions.

Scalloped Potatoes

Hope Comerford, Clinton Township, MI

Makes 8–10 servings
Prep. Time: 15 minutes ⚜ Cooking Time: 1 minute ⚜ Baking Time: 15 minutes

3 lb. white potatoes, peeled or unpeeled and sliced into 4-inch-thick slices, *divided*

1 cup chicken broth

1 tsp. garlic powder

½ tsp. salt

¼ tsp. pepper

½ cup heavy cream

Nonstick cooking spray

¼ lb. bacon, cut in 1-inch squares, browned until crisp, and drained, *divided*

2 cups shredded cheddar cheese, *divided*

1. Place the potato slices, broth, garlic powder, salt, and pepper in the inner pot of the Instant Pot.

2. Secure the lid and set the vent to sealing. Manually set the cook time for 1 minutes.

3. When the cook time is over, let the pressure release naturally for 3 minutes, then manually release the remaining pressure.

4. When the pin drops, remove the lid. Drain the potatoes, reserving the liquid. Set the potatoes aside for a moment, and return the liquid back to the inner pot.

5. Set the Instant Pot to the Sauté function. Stir in the heavy cream. Let the mixture simmer for a couple minutes.

6. Preheat the oven to 375°F.

7. Spray a 7-inch round baking dish or pie dish with nonstick cooking spray. Layer in half of the potatoes, half of the bacon, half of the cheese, and half of the cream sauce. Repeat this process with the remaining potatoes, bacon, cheese, and sauce.

8. Place the baking dish into the oven for 15 minutes, or until bubbly.

Mashed Potatoes

Colleen Heatwole, Burton, MI

Makes 3–4 servings
Prep. Time: 10 minutes   Cooking Time: 5 minutes

1 cup water

6 medium potatoes, peeled and quartered

2 Tbsp. unsalted butter

½ to ¾ cup milk, warmed

Salt to taste

Pepper to taste

1. Add the water to the inner pot of the Instant Pot. Put the steamer basket in the pot and place the potatoes in the basket.

2. Seal the lid and make sure the vent is on sealing. Manually set the cook time for 5 minutes on high pressure.

3. When cook time ends, manually release the pressure. Use a fork to test the potatoes. If needed, relock the lid and cook at high pressure a few minutes more.

4. Transfer the potatoes to a large mixing bowl. Mash using a hand mixer, stirring in the butter. Gradually add the warmed milk. Season with salt and pepper to taste.

Creamy Red Potato Salad

Hope Comerford, Clinton Township, MI

Makes 10–15 servings
Prep. Time: 20 minutes ⚬ Cooking Time: 4 minutes

I cup water

2 lb. red potatoes, washed and cut into ¾-inch pieces (skin on or off)

3 eggs, washed

Dressing:

3 cooked egg yolks (from the eggs you cooked in the Instant Pot)

½ cup mayonnaise

2 tsp. red wine vinegar

I tsp. Dijon mustard

½ tsp. sugar

½ tsp. salt

½ tsp. garlic powder

¼ tsp. pepper

¼ cup crumbled bacon

¼ cup diced celery

¼ cup diced green onions

3 egg whites, chopped (from the eggs cooked in the Instant Pot)

1. Pour the cup of water into the inner pot of the Instant Pot, then place the steamer basket inside.

2. Place the potato pieces and eggs into the steamer basket.

3. Secure the lid and set the vent to sealing.

4. Manually set the cook time for 4 minutes.

5. When cook time is up, manually release the pressure.

6. Place the 3 eggs into a bowl of ice water to stop the cooking process.

7. Remove potatoes and place them in a large bowl to cool.

8. Once the eggs are cooled, peel them, slice them in half width-wise, remove the egg yolks and set aside. Chop up the egg whites and set aside, separately from the yolks.

9. In a small bowl, mix the mashed egg yolks, mayonnaise, red wine vinegar, mustard, sugar, salt, garlic powder, and pepper. Stir in the bacon, celery, green onions, and egg whites.

10. Pour the dressing over the cooled potatoes and gently stir to coat everything evenly. Refrigerate or serve warm, depending on how you like it.

Sweet Potato Puree

Colleen Heatwole, Burton, MI

Makes 4–6 servings
Prep. Time: 10 minutes ❧ Cooking Time: 6 minutes

3 lb. sweet potatoes, peeled and cut into roughly 2-inch cubes

1 cup water

2 Tbsp. butter

1 tsp. salt

2 tsp. packed brown sugar

2 tsp. lemon juice

½ tsp. cinnamon

⅛ tsp. nutmeg, *optional*

1. Place the sweet potatoes and water in the inner pot of the Instant Pot.

2. Secure the lid, make sure the vent is on sealing, then manually set the cook time for 6 minutes on high pressure.

3. Manually release the pressure when the cook time is over.

4. Drain the sweet potatoes and place them in a large mixing bowl. Mash with a potato masher or hand mixer.

5. Once thoroughly mashed, add remaining ingredients.

6. Taste and adjust seasonings to taste.

7. Serve immediately while still hot.

Cilantro Lime Rice

Cindy Herren, West Des Moines, IA

Makes 6–8 servings
Prep. Time: 5 minutes ⚖ *Cooking Time: 3 minutes*

2 cups extra-long grain rice or jasmine rice

4 cup water

2 Tbsp. olive oil or butter, *divided*

2 tsp. salt

¼ cup fresh chopped cilantro

1 lime, juiced

1. Add the rice, the water, 1 Tbsp. of the oil, and the salt to the inner pot of the Instant Pot and stir.

2. Secure the lid and set the vent to sealing.

3. Manually set the cook time to 3 minutes on high pressure.

4. When the cooking time is over, let the pressure release naturally for 10 minutes, then manually release the remaining pressure.

5. When the pin drops, remove the lid. Fluff the rice with a fork. Add the chopped cilantro, lime juice, and remaining oil and mix well.

Hometown Spanish Rice

Beverly Flatt-Getz, Warriors Mark, PA

Makes 6–8 servings
Prep. Time: 8 minutes ❧ *Cooking Time: 3 minutes*

1 Tbsp. olive oil

1 large onion, chopped

1 bell pepper, chopped

2 cups long-grain rice, rinsed

1½ cups low-sodium chicken stock

28-oz. can low-sodium stewed tomatoes

Grated Parmesan cheese, *optional*

1. Set the Instant Pot to Sauté and heat the oil in the inner pot.

2. Sauté the onion and bell pepper in the inner pot for about 3 to 5 minutes.

3. Add the rice and continue to sauté for about 1 more minute. Press Cancel.

4. Add the chicken stock and tomatoes with their juices into the inner pot, in that order.

5. Secure the lid and set the vent to sealing.

6. Manually set the cook time for 3 minutes on high pressure.

7. When the cooking time is over, let the pressure release naturally for 10 minutes, then manually release the remaining pressure.

8. When the pin drops, remove the lid. Fluff the rice with a fork.

9. Sprinkle with Parmesan cheese, if using, just before serving.

Cheesy Broccoli Rice Casserole

Hope Comerford, Clinton Township, MI

Makes 4 servings
Prep. Time: 10 minutes ❧ Cooking Time: 6 minutes

1 Tbsp. olive oil
¾ cup chopped onion
4-oz. fresh sliced mushrooms
2 cups rice
1 tsp. garlic powder
1 tsp. salt
¼ tsp. pepper
2½ cups chicken broth, *divided*
2 cups chopped broccoli florets
1½ cups shredded cheddar cheese

1. Set the Instant Pot to Sauté mode and heat the oil.

2. Sauté the onion and mushrooms in the oil for about 3 minutes. Press Cancel.

3. Add the rice, garlic powder, salt, pepper, and 2 cups of the broth. Stir.

4. Secure the lid and set the vent to sealing. Manually set the cook time for 5 minutes on high pressure.

5. When the cook time is over, manually release the pressure. When the pin drops remove the lid.

6. Stir in the broccoli and remaining ½ cup of broth.

7. Secure the lid and set the vent to sealing. Manually set the cook time for 1 minute on high pressure.

8. When the cook time is over, manually release the pressure.

9. When the pin drops, remove the lid, and stir in the cheese.

Veggie Loaded Rice

Maria Shevlin, Sicklerville, NJ

Makes 4–6 servings
Prep. Time: 10 minutes ⚬ Cooking Time: 3–5 minutes

1 Tbsp. olive oil
2–3 cloves garlic, minced
½ medium onion, chopped fine
½ cup carrot, shredded
¼ cup red bell pepper, chopped fine
½ cup mushrooms, chopped fine
½ cup zucchini, shredded
2 cups cooked rice, warmed
½ cup vegetable stock
1 tsp. salt
½ tsp. garlic powder
¼ tsp. onion powder
½ tsp. black pepper
1–2 pinches red pepper flakes
1 Tbsp. fresh parsley, chopped fine
2 tsp. fresh basil, chiffonade

1. Set the Instant Pot to Sauté and add the oil to heat.

2. Sauté the garlic, onion, carrot, and bell pepper for 3–5 minutes, stirring frequently.

3. Add the mushrooms and zucchini and stir until mixed.

4. Press Cancel. Add the rice, stock, and seasonings. Mix well, taste and adjust salt and pepper if needed.

5. Stir in the fresh herbs.

Serving suggestions:

Serve as a main course or side dish to chicken, pork, or beef.

You can even add in cooked shrimp and a couple of scrambled eggs for a shrimp & veggie fried rice–style meal.

Baked Beans

Hope Comerford, Clinton Township, MI

Makes 20 or more servings
Prep. Time: 10 minutes ❧ Cooking Time: 60 minutes

16 oz. navy beans, rinsed

9½ cups water, *divided*

12 oz. salt pork, chopped into small strips

1 large onion, chopped

1 cup ketchup

¾ cup dark brown sugar

3 Tbsp. mustard

Note:
These will thicken as they cool.

1. Place the navy beans and 9 cups water in the inner pot of the Instant Pot.

2. Secure the lid and set the vent to sealing. Manually set the cook time for 15 minutes on high pressure.

3. When the cook time is over, let the pressure release naturally for 20 minutes, then manually release the remaining pressure.

4. When the pin drops, remove the lid. Drain and rinse the beans. Rinse out the inner pot and wipe it dry.

5. Set the Instant Pot to the Sauté function. Let it get very hot, then add the salt pork. Sauté for a few minutes, and when the fat really starts to render, add the onion and continue to sauté for a couple more minutes.

6. Pour in ½ cup of water and scrape up any bits from the bottom with a wooden spatula or spoon. Press Cancel.

7. Mix the ketchup, brown sugar, and mustard.

8. Pour the remaining water into the inner pot. Add half the beans, then half of the ketchup sauce. Finish with the remaining beans and ketchup sauce.

9. Secure the lid and set the vent to sealing. Manually set the cook time for 35 minutes.

10. When the cook time is over, let the pressure release naturally for 20 minutes, then manually release the remaining pressure.

11. When the pin drops, remove the lid and stir the beans. Press Cancel.

Perfect Pinto Beans

Hope Comerford, Clinton Township, MI

Makes 8 servings
Prep. Time: 2 minutes   ⚶   Cooking Time: 50 minutes

I large onion, chopped

I lb. dry pinto beans, sorted and rinsed

6 cups vegetable or chicken broth

2 bay leaves

I ½ tsp. sea salt

I tsp. cumin

½ tsp. paprika

¼ tsp. pepper

1. Place all ingredients into the inner pot of the Instant Pot.

2. Secure the lid and set the vent to sealing. Manually set the cook time for 50 minutes on high pressure.

3. When the cook time is over, let the pressure release naturally for 15 minutes, then manually release the remaining pressure. Remove and discard bay leaves before serving.

Corn on the Cob

Hope Comerford, Clinton Township, MI

Makes 6 servings
Prep. Time: 10 minutes & *Cooking Time: 2 minutes*

1 cup water

6 small ears of corn, husked and ends cut off

1. Place the trivet in the bottom of the Instant Pot and pour in the water.

2. Place the ears of corn inside.

3. Seal the lid and make sure vent is set to sealing. Press Manual and set time for 2 minutes.

4. When cook time is up, release the pressure manually.

Serving suggestion:
Sprinkle with finely chopped fresh herbs and/or paprika.

Creamed Corn

Hope Comerford, Clinton Township, MI

Makes 6 servings
Prep. Time: 5 minutes ⚶ Cooking Time: 3 minutes

8 oz. cream cheese, cubed

1 stick butter, chopped into tablespoons

24 oz. frozen corn

1 Tbsp. sugar

¼ tsp. dried mustard

¼ tsp. salt

⅛ tsp. pepper

1. Place all ingredients into the inner pot of the Instant Pot as listed.

2. Secure the lid and set the vent to sealing.

3. Manually set the cook time for 3 minutes.

4. When cook time is up, manually release the pressure.

5. Remove the lid, stir, and enjoy!

Variations:

You can use different flavored cream cheeses to change the flavor of your creamed corn.

You can add in diced green chilies or jalapeños to give your creamed corn a kick!

You can add crumbled cooked bacon for some extra goodness!

Brown Sugar Glazed Carrots

Michele Ruvola, Vestal, NY

Makes 10 servings

Prep. Time: 5 minutes & *Cooking Time: 4 minutes*

32-oz. bag of baby carrots
½ cup vegetable broth
½ cup brown sugar
4 Tbsp. butter
½ Tbsp. salt

1. Place all ingredients in inner pot of the Instant Pot.

2. Secure the lid and set the vent to sealing. Manually set the cook time for 4 minutes on high pressure.

3. When cooking time is up, manually release the pressure.

4. When the pin drops remove the lid. Stir the carrots, then serve.

Rosemary Carrots

Orpha Herr, Andover, NY

Makes 6 servings

Prep. Time: 10 minutes ❧ *Cooking Time: 2 minutes*

I cup water

I ½ lb. carrots, sliced

I Tbsp. olive oil

½ cup diced green bell pepper

I tsp. dried rosemary, crushed

¼ tsp. coarsely ground black pepper

1. Pour the water into the inner pot of the Instant Pot, place the sliced carrots into a steamer basket, and put the steamer basket into the inner pot.

2. Secure the lid and set the vent to sealing.

3. Manually set the cook time for 2 minutes on high pressure.

4. When the cooking time is over, manually release the pressure. Wait for the pin to drop and remove the lid. Press Cancel.

5. Carefully remove the carrots, set aside, and empty the water out of the inner pot. Wipe dry.

6. Place the inner pot back into the Instant Pot, then press Sauté and heat the oil in the inner pot.

7. Add the green bell pepper and sauté for 5 minutes, then add the carrots and stir.

8. Sprinkle the carrots and green pepper with rosemary and black pepper. Serve and enjoy!

Broccoli with Garlic

Andrea Cunningham, Arlington, KS

Makes 4 servings

Prep. Time: 5 minutes ⁂ *Cooking Time: 2–3 minutes*

½ cup cold water

I head (about 5 cups) broccoli, cut into long pieces all the way through (you will eat the stems)

I Tbsp. olive oil

2–3 cloves garlic, sliced thin

⅛ tsp. pepper

Lemon wedges to taste

1. Place a steamer basket into the inner pot along with the ½ cup cold water. Put the broccoli into the steamer basket.

2. Secure the lid and set the vent to sealing.

3. Manually set the cook time for 0 minutes on high pressure.

4. Manually release the pressure when it's done. Press Cancel.

5. When the pin drops, open the lid and place the broccoli into an ice bath or run under cold water to stop it from cooking. Let it air dry.

6. Carefully remove the water from the inner pot and wipe it dry.

7. Set the Instant Pot to the Sauté function and heat the oil.

8. Sauté the garlic for 1 minute, then add the broccoli, sprinkle it with the pepper, and continue to sauté for an additional 1 to 2 minutes.

9. Just before serving, squeeze lemon juice over the top.

Steamed Veggie Medley

Maria Shevlin, Sicklerville, NJ

Makes 6 servings
Prep. Time: 5 minutes   Cooking Time: 2 minutes

1 cup water
3 cups fresh cauliflower florets
16-oz. bag baby carrots, cut in half
1 Tbsp. olive oil
2 Tbsp. butter
8 oz. mushrooms, diced
1 small onion, diced
2 cloves garlic, minced
salt and pepper to taste
½ tsp. garlic powder
2 Tbsp. fresh parsley, chopped
½ tsp. fresh thyme, chopped fine
½ tsp. fresh sage, chopped fine

1. Pour 1 cup water into the bottom of the inner pot. Place the steamer basket inside.

2. Add in the cauliflower and carrots.

3. Secure the lid and set the vent to sealing. Press Steam and set the timer to 2 minutes.

4. When cook time is up, let the pressure release naturally for 3–4 minutes, then manually release any remaining pressure.

5. When the pin drops, remove the lid, and carefully lift the steamer basket out. Drain the water from the pot and cover the veggies to keep them warm.

6. Press Sauté, then add the olive oil, butter, mushrooms, onions, and garlic to the inner pot.

7. Sauté until the veggies are cooked, then press Cancel. Add the steamed cauliflower and carrots in and toss together.

8. Season with salt, pepper, and garlic powder.

9. Top with the fresh herbs and toss gently.

Serving suggestions:
For a vegetarian style meal, serve over quinoa, couscous, or rice.

Makes a great side to any protein.

Green Bean Casserole

Hope Comerford, Clinton Township, MI

Makes 6 servings
Prep. Time: 5 minutes · Cooking Time: 2 minutes

2 (14½-oz.) cans French-cut green beans, drained

⅔ cup vegetable broth

6 oz. container french-fried onions, *divided*

1 tsp. soy sauce

½ tsp. Worcestershire sauce

1 tsp. garlic powder

⅛ tsp. pepper

10¾-oz. can condensed cream of mushroom soup

¼ cup sour cream

1. Place the green beans, vegetable broth, ⅓ cup of the french-fried onions, soy sauce, Worcestershire sauce, garlic powder, and pepper into the inner pot of the Instant Pot.

2. Spread the cream of mushroom soup over the top.

3. Secure the lid and set the vent to sealing. Manually set the cook time for 2 minutes on high pressure.

4. When the cook time is over, manually release the pressure.

5. When the pin drops, remove the lid and stir in the sour cream. Once combined, pour the remaining french-fried onions over the top. Let it sit for a few minutes to thicken up.

Brussels Sprouts with Maple Glaze

Hope Comerford, Clinton Township, MI

Makes 6 servings
Prep. Time: 5–6 minutes ❧ *Cook Time: 3 minutes*

Nonstick cooking spray
4 slices thick-cut bacon, chopped
I shallot, diced
½ cup chicken broth
I lb. Brussels sprouts, halved if large
⅓ cup light brown sugar
1½ Tbsp. Dijon mustard
2 Tbsp. maple syrup

1. Set the Instant Pot to the Sauté function and let it get nice and hot. Spray the inner pot with nonstick cooking spray and then add the bacon. Sauté until crispy.

2. Add the shallot and sauté for 1 more minute.

3. Pour in the chicken broth and scrape the bottom of the pot with a wooden spoon or spatula. Press Cancel.

4. Pour in the Brussels sprouts and secure the lid. Set the vent to sealing.

5. Manually set the cook time for 3 minutes. When the cook time is over, manually release the pressure.

6. When the pin drops, remove the lid.

7. In a medium bowl, mix together the brown sugar, Dijon mustard, and maple syrup.

8. Remove the contents of the inner pot with a slotted spoon into the bowl with the maple glaze. Toss and serve.

Sour Cream Corn Bread

Edwina Stoltzfus, Narvon, PA

Makes 9 servings
Prep. Time: 10 minutes   *Cooking Time: 55 minutes*

2 egg whites, beaten
¼ cup skim milk
2 Tbsp. canola oil
1 cup sour cream
¾ cup cornmeal
½ cup whole wheat flour
½ cup all-purpose flour
¼ cup turbinado sugar, or sugar of your choice
2 tsp. baking powder
½ tsp. baking soda
Nonstick cooking spray
1 cup water

1. Place the egg whites in a large mixing bowl and beat.

2. Add the milk, oil, and sour cream and combine well.

3. In a separate bowl, combine all dry ingredients.

4. Add the dry ingredients to the wet ones. Mix together just until moistened.

5. Spoon into a 7 x 3-inch round baking pan sprayed lightly with nonstick cooking spray. Wrap the top tightly with foil, then take a second piece of foil and wrap the bottom, too.

6. Pour the water into the inner pot of the Instant Pot. Place the trivet on top.

7. Place the foil-wrapped baking pan on the trivet. Secure the lid and set the vent to sealing.

8. Manually set the time to cook for 55 minutes on high pressure.

9. When the cook time is over, let the pressure release naturally for 10 minutes, then manually release the remaining pressure.

10. Carefully remove the trivet with oven mitts. Wipe any moisture off of the foil, then carefully remove the foil from the pan.

11. Serve warm!

Desserts

Brownie Bites

Hope Comerford, Clinton Township, MI

Makes 14 brownie bites
Prep. Time: 5 minutes ❧ Cooking Time: 25–30 minutes

Nonstick cooking spray
½ cup all-purpose flour
½ cup unsweetened cocoa powder
1 tsp. baking powder
1 cup turbinado sugar
2 eggs
1 stick of butter, melted
1 tsp. vanilla extract
¼ cup plus 2 Tbsp. milk
1 cup water

1. Spray 2 silicone egg bite molds with nonstick spray.

2. Mix the flour, cocoa powder, baking powder, and sugar in a bowl.

3. Add the eggs, butter, vanilla, and milk to the dry ingredients and mix well.

4. Evenly divide the batter into the egg bite molds (no more than ⅔ of the way full).

5. Cover each egg bite mold with paper towel and then foil.

6. Place the trivet with handles into the inner pot of the Instant Pot, then pour in the cup of water.

7. Stack the 2 silicone egg molds on top of the trivet in the Inner Pot.

8. Seal the lid and set the vent to sealing.

9. Manually set the cook time for 25–30 minutes, depending on how gooey or firm you like your brownies.

10. When cook time is up, let the pressure release naturally for 10 minutes, then manually release the rest.

11. Carefully remove the trivet with the handles and let the brownie bites sit, uncovered, for about 10 minutes to cool and set before eating or serving.

Chocolate Bundt Cake

Margaret Wenger Johnson, Keezletown, VA

Makes 10 servings
Prep. Time: 15 minutes ⚘ *Cooking Time: 30 minutes* ⚘ *Cooling Time: 20 minutes*

1½ cups whole wheat pastry flour

½ cup turbinado sugar, or sugar of your choice

1½ Tbsp. unsweetened cocoa powder

¼ tsp. salt

1⅛ tsp. baking soda

½ Tbsp. vanilla extract

1 Tbsp. white vinegar

¼ cup canola oil

1 cup boiling water

1 cup room-temperature water

1. In a mixing bowl, sift together the flour, sugar, cocoa powder, salt, and baking soda.

2. Make 3 holes in the dry ingredients. Pour the vanilla, vinegar, and oil into those holes.

3. Add the boiling water. Beat for 2 minutes by hand, or with a mixer. (This will make a thin batter.)

4. Pour the batter into a greased 7-inch nonstick Bundt pan. Cover with foil.

5. Pour the room-temperature water into the inner pot of the Instant Pot and place the trivet on top.

6. Place the covered Bundt pan on top of the trivet in the inner pot. Secure the lid and set the vent to sealing.

7. Manually set the cook time for 30 minutes on high pressure.

8. When the cooking time is over, let the pressure release naturally.

9. When the pin drops, remove the lid and carefully remove the trivet with oven mitts.

10. Remove the foil and let the cake cool for about 20 minutes.

Cherry Delight Dump Cake

Janice Muller, Derwood, MD

Makes 15 servings
Prep. Time: 20 minutes ☙ Cooking Time: 50 minutes

Nonstick cooking spray

20-oz. can crushed pineapple

21-oz. can blueberry or cherry pie filling

18½-oz. package yellow cake mix

cinnamon

⅓ cup light, soft tub margarine

⅓ cup chopped walnuts

1 cup water

Variation:

Use a package of spice cake mix and apple pie filling.

1. Grease the bottom and sides of a 7-inch springform pan.

2. Spread layers of pineapple, blueberry pie filling, and dry cake mix. Be careful not to mix the layers.

3. Sprinkle with cinnamon.

4. Top with thin layers of margarine chunks and nuts.

5. Cover the pan with foil.

6. Place the trivet into the Instant Pot and pour in the water. Place a foil sling on top of the trivet, then place the springform pan on top.

7. Secure the lid and make sure lid is set to sealing. Press Steam and set for 50 minutes.

8. When the cook time is over, release the pressure manually, then carefully remove the springform pan by using hot pads to lift the pan up by the foil sling. Place on a cooling rack until cool.

Carrot Cake

Colleen Heatwole, Burton, MI

Makes 10 servings
Prep. Time: 35 minutes ♧ Cooking Time: 50 minutes

⅓ cup canola oil

2 eggs

1 Tbsp. hot water

½ cup grated raw carrots

¾ cup flour and 2 Tbsp. flour, *divided*

¾ cup sugar

½ tsp. baking powder

⅛ tsp. salt

¼ tsp. ground allspice

½ tsp. ground cinnamon

⅛ tsp. ground cloves

½ cup chopped nuts

½ cup raisins or chopped dates

1 cup water

1. In a large bowl, beat the oil, eggs, and water for 1 minute.

2. Add the carrots. Mix well.

3. In another bowl, stir together the ¾ cup flour, sugar, baking powder, salt, allspice, cinnamon, and cloves. Add to the creamed mixture.

4. Toss the nuts and raisins in a bowl with 2 Tbsp. of flour. Add to creamed mixture. Mix well.

5. Pour into greased and floured 7-inch springform pan and cover with foil.

6. Place the trivet into the Instant Pot and pour in the water. Place a foil sling on top of the trivet, then place the springform pan on top.

7. Secure the lid and make sure lid is set to sealing. Press Steam and set for 50 minutes.

8. When the cook time is over, release the pressure manually, then carefully remove the springform pan by using hot pads to lift the pan up by the foil sling. Place on a cooling rack until cool.

Strawberry Shortcake

Joanna Harrison, Lafayette, CO

Makes 8 servings

Prep. Time: 25 minutes ⚬ *Cooking Time: 40 minutes* ⚬ *Cooling Time: 7 minutes*

1 qt. (4 cups) fresh strawberries

3 Tbsp. honey, *divided*

1½ cups whole wheat pastry flour

1 tsp. baking powder

⅛ tsp. salt

¼ cup butter

2 egg whites

½ cup milk

1 cup water

1. Mash or slice the strawberries in a bowl. Stir in 2 Tbsp. honey. Set aside and refrigerate.

2. In a large mixing bowl, combine the flour, baking powder, salt, and 1 Tbsp. honey.

3. Cut the butter into the dry ingredients with a pastry cutter or 2 knives until crumbly.

4. In a small bowl, beat the egg whites and milk together.

5. Stir the wet ingredients into the flour mixture just until moistened.

6. Pour the batter into a greased 7-inch Bundt pan. Cover tightly with foil.

7. Pour the water into the inner pot and place the trivet on top. Place the Bundt pan on top of the trivet in the inner pot. Secure the lid and set the vent to sealing.

8. Manually set the cook time for 40 minutes on high pressure.

9. When cooking time is up, allow the pressure to release naturally for 10 minutes, then manually release the remaining pressure.

10. When the pin drops, remove the lid and carefully lift the trivet out of the inner pot with oven mitts.

11. Allow cake to cool in the pan for 7 minutes, then remove onto the cooling rack.

12. Cut the cake into desired servings and spoon berries over the top.

Black and Blue Cobbler

Renee Shirk, Mount Joy, PA

Makes 12 servings
Prep. Time: 30 minutes ⚘ Cooking Time: 35 minutes ⚘ Cooling Time: 30 minutes

1 cup flour
1½ cups sugar, *divided*
1 tsp. baking powder
¼ tsp. salt
¼ tsp. ground cinnamon
¼ tsp. ground nutmeg
2 eggs, beaten
2 Tbsp. milk
2 Tbsp. vegetable oil
2 cups fresh, or frozen, blueberries
2 cups fresh, or frozen, blackberries
¾ cup water
1 tsp. grated orange peel
1 cup water
Whipped topping or ice cream, *optional*

1. Combine flour, ¾ cup sugar, baking powder, salt, cinnamon, and nutmeg.

2. Combine eggs, milk, and oil. Stir into dry ingredients until moistened.

3. Spread the batter evenly over bottom of greased 1½-quart baking dish.

4. In saucepan, combine berries, ¾ cup water, orange peel, and the remaining ¾ cup sugar. Bring to boil. Remove from heat and pour over batter. Cover with foil.

5. Place the trivet into your Instant Pot and pour in 1 cup of water. Place a foil sling on top of the trivet, then place the baking dish on top.

6. Secure the lid and make sure lid is set to sealing. Press Manual and set for 35 minutes.

7. When cook time is up, allow the pressure to release naturally for 10 minutes, then release the remaining pressure manually. Carefully remove the baking dish by using hot pads to lift the foil sling. Place on a cooling rack, uncovered, for 30 minutes.

8. Serve with optional whipped topping or ice cream.

Quick and Yummy Peach Cobbler

Willard E. Roth, Elkhart, IN

Makes 8 servings

Prep. Time: 10 minutes ⚬ *Cooking Time: 10 minutes* ⚬ *Cooling Time: 20–30 minutes*

⅓ cup buttermilk baking mix

⅔ cup dry quick oats

6 Tbsp. brown sugar

1 tsp. cinnamon

4 cups sliced peaches, canned or fresh

½ cup peach juice or water

1 cup water

1. Mix together baking mix, oats, brown sugar, and cinnamon. Mix in the peaches and peach juice.

2. Pour mixture into a 1½-quart baking dish. Cover with foil.

3. Place the trivet into your Instant Pot and pour in 1 cup of water. Place a foil sling on top of the trivet, then place the baking dish on top.

4. Secure the lid and make sure lid is set to sealing. Press Manual and set for 10 minutes.

5. When cook time is up, let the pressure release naturally for 10 minutes, then release any remaining pressure manually. Carefully remove the baking dish by using hot pads to lift the foil sling. Uncover and let cool for about 20–30 minutes.

Coconut Rice Pudding

Hope Comerford, Clinton Township, MI

Makes 6 servings

Prep. Time: 2 minutes ☆ Cooking Time: 10 minutes

1 cup arborio rice, rinsed

1 cup unsweetened almond milk

14-oz. can light coconut milk

½ cup water

½ cup turbinado sugar, or sugar of
your choice

1 stick cinnamon

¼ cup dried cranberries, *optional*

¼ cup unsweetened coconut flakes,
optional

1. Place the rice into the inner pot of the Instant pot, along with all the remaining ingredients except the cranberries and coconut flakes.

2. Secure the lid and set the vent to sealing.

3. Using the Porridge setting, set the cook time for 10 minutes.

4. When the cooking time is over, let the pressure release naturally.

5. When the pin drops, remove the lid and remove cinnamon stick.

6. Stir and serve as is or sprinkle some cranberries and unsweetened coconut flakes on top of each serving. Enjoy!

Banana Bread Bites

Hope Comerford, Clinton Township, MI

Makes 14 banana bread bites
Prep. Time: 10 minutes   Cooking Time: 10 minutes

1½ cups gluten-free cup-for-cup flour

½ cup gluten-free old-fashioned oats

1 tsp. baking soda

½ tsp. cinnamon

¼ tsp. nutmeg

¼ tsp. salt

3 very ripe bananas, mashed

⅓ cup unsweetened applesauce

½ cup honey

2 eggs

1 tsp. vanilla extract

Nonstick cooking spray

1 cup water

1. In a bowl, mix the flour, oats, baking soda, cinnamon, nutmeg, and salt.

2. In a separate bowl, mix the mashed bananas, applesauce, honey, eggs, and vanilla.

3. Mix the wet ingredients into the dry ingredients, only until just combined. Do not overmix.

4. Spray 2 silicone egg bite molds with nonstick cooking spray.

5. Fill each mold ¾ of the way full of batter. Cover the molds with foil.

6. Pour the water into the inner pot of the Instant Pot.

7. Stack both filled silicone molds onto the trivet and carefully lower the trivet into the inner pot.

8. Secure the lid and set the vent to sealing.

9. Manually select 10 minutes of cooking time on high pressure.

10. When the cooking time is over, let the pressure release naturally for 5 minutes, then manually release the remaining pressure.

11. Remove the lid and carefully lift the trivet and molds out of the pot with oven mitts.

12. Remove the foil and allow the banana bread bites to cool. Pop them out of the molds onto a plate or serving platter.

Caramel Corn

Hope Comerford, Clinton Township, MI

Makes 5–6 servings
Prep. Time: 3 minutes   Cook Time: 15 minutes

2 Tbsp. coconut oil

½ cup popcorn kernels

½ tsp. sea salt

Caramel sauce:

½ cup sweet cream salted butter

½ cup light brown sugar

2 Tbsp. heavy cream

I tsp. vanilla extract

¼ tsp. baking soda

1. Set the Instant Pot to the Sauté function. Add the coconut oil and let it melt.

2. When the oil is melted, add the popcorn kernels, stir, then secure the lid. Let it cook for about 3 minutes, or until you do not hear kernels popping.

3. Press Cancel and move the popcorn to a bowl. Toss with the salt.

4. Place the inner pot back into the Instant Pot base and press the Sauté function.

5. Add the butter and let it melt. Once it's melted, add the brown sugar and heavy cream. When the sugar is dissolved add the vanilla and baking soda. Continue to cook until the sauce has thickened into caramel. This should all take about 12 minutes.

6. Press Cancel on the Instant Pot. Add the popcorn back into the inner pot and gently stir to coat it with the caramel sauce.

7. Line a baking sheet with parchment paper, foil, or a silicone mat. Pour the caramel corn onto the baking sheet in a single layer and let it cool.

Cookies & Cream Cheesecake (Gluten-Free)

Hope Comerford, Clinton Township, MI

Makes 6 servings
Prep. Time: 15 minutes ⚶ *Cooking Time: 35 minutes*

Nonstick cooking spray

Crust:

12 whole gluten-free chocolate sandwich cookies, crushed into crumbs

2 Tbsp. salted butter, melted

Cheesecake:

16 oz. cream cheese, room temperature

½ cup granulated sugar

2 large eggs, room temperature

1 Tbsp. gluten-free all-purpose flour

¼ cup heavy cream

2 tsp. pure vanilla extract

8 whole gluten-free chocolate sandwich cookies, coarsely chopped

Toppings:

1 cup whipped cream

chopped gluten-free chocolate sandwich cookies, *optional*

chocolate sauce, *optional*

1. Tightly wrap in foil the bottom of 7-inch springform pan. Spray the inside with nonstick cooking spray.

2. In a small bowl, stir together the 12 crushed gluten-free chocolate sandwich cookies and melted butter. Press the crumbs into the bottom of the prepared pan. (I find the bottom of a glass cup is a great tool to use for this.) Place this in the freezer for 10–15 minutes.

3. In a large bowl, beat the cream cheese until smooth. (You can use an electric mixer, or a stand mixer with paddle attachment.)

4. Add the sugar and mix until combined.

5. Add the eggs, one at a time, making sure each is fully incorporated before adding the next. Be sure to scrape down the bowl in between each egg.

6. Add in the flour, heavy cream, and vanilla and continue to mix until smooth.

7. Gently fold in the 8 chopped gluten-free chocolate sandwich cookies and pour this batter into the pan you had in the freezer.

8. Cover the top of the pan with a piece of foil.

9. Pour 1½ cups of water into the inner pot and place the trivet in the bottom of the pot.

(Continued on next page)

10. Create a "foil sling" by folding a 20-inch long piece of foil in half lengthwise two times. This "sling" will allow you to easily place and remove the springform pan from the pot.

11. Place the cheesecake pan in the center of the sling and carefully lower the pan into the inner pot. Fold down the excess foil from the sling to ensure the pot closes properly.

12. Lock the lid into place and make sure the vent is at sealing. Press the Manual button and cook on high pressure for 35 minutes.

13. When the Instant Pot beeps, hit the Keep Warm/Cancel button to turn off the pressure cooker. Allow the pressure to release naturally for 10 minutes and then do a quick release to release any pressure remaining in the pot.

14. Carefully remove the lid. Gently unfold the foil sling and remove the cheesecake from the pot to a cooling rack using the foil sling "handles." Uncover the cheesecake and allow it to cool to room temperature.

15. Once the cheesecake has cooled, refrigerate it for at least 8 hours, or overnight.

16. Before serving, top with whipped cream, chopped gluten-free chocolate sandwich cookies, and a drizzle of chocolate sauce if desired.

Metric Equivalent Measurements

If you're accustomed to using metric measurements, I don't want you to be inconvenienced by the imperial measurements I use in this book.

Use this handy chart, too, to figure out the size of the slow cooker you'll need for each recipe.

Weight (Dry Ingredients)

1 oz		30 g
4 oz	¼ lb	120 g
8 oz	½ lb	240 g
12 oz	¾ lb	360 g
16 oz	1 lb	480 g
32 oz	2 lb	960 g

Slow-Cooker Sizes

1-quart	0.96 l
2-quart	1.92 l
3-quart	2.88 l
4-quart	3.84 l
5-quart	4.80 l
6-quart	5.76 l
7-quart	6.72 l
8-quart	7.68 l

Volume (Liquid Ingredients)

½ tsp.		2 ml
1 tsp.		5 ml
1 Tbsp.	½ fl oz	15 ml
2 Tbsp.	1 fl oz	30 ml
¼ cup	2 fl oz	60 ml
⅓ cup	3 fl oz	80 ml
½ cup	4 fl oz	120 ml
⅔ cup	5 fl oz	160 ml
¾ cup	6 fl oz	180 ml
1 cup	8 fl oz	240 ml
1 pt	16 fl oz	480 ml
1 qt	32 fl oz	960 ml

Length

¼ in	6 mm
½ in	13 mm
¾ in	19 mm
1 in	25 mm
6 in	15 cm
12 in	30 cm

Recipe and Ingredient Index

About the Author

Hope Comerford is a mom, wife, elementary music teacher, blogger, recipe developer, public speaker, Young Living Essential Oils essential oil enthusiast/educator, and published author. In 2013, she was diagnosed with a severe gluten intolerance and since then has spent many hours creating easy, practical and delicious gluten-free recipes that can be enjoyed by both those who are affected by gluten and those who are not.

Growing up, Hope spent many hours in the kitchen with her Meme (grandmother) and her love for cooking grew from there. While working on her master's degree when her daughter was young, Hope turned to her slow cookers for some salvation and sanity. It was from there she began truly experimenting with recipes and quickly learned she had the ability to get a little more creative in the kitchen and develop her own recipes.

In 2010, Hope started her blog, *A Busy Mom's Slow Cooker Adventures*, to simply share the recipes she was making with her family and friends. She never imagined people all over the world would begin visiting her page and sharing her recipes with others as well. In 2013, Hope self-published her first cookbook, *Slow Cooker Recipes 10 Ingredients or Less and Gluten-Free*, and then later wrote *The Gluten-Free Slow Cooker*.

Hope became the new brand ambassador and author of Fix-It and Forget-It in mid-2016. Since then, she has brought her excitement and creativeness to the Fix-It and Forget-It brand. Through Fix-It and Forget-It, she has written *Fix-It and Forget-It Healthy Slow Cooker Cookbook*, *Fix-It and Forget-It Healthy 5-Ingredient Cookbook*, *Fix-It and Forget-It Instant Pot Cookbook*, *Fix-It and Forget-It Plant-Based Comfort Foods Cookbook*, *Welcome Home Harvest Cookbook*, *Welcome Home Pies, Crisps and Crumbles*, *Fix-It and Forget-It Instant Pot Light & Healthy Cookbook*, and many more.

Hope lives in the city of Clinton Township, Michigan, near Metro Detroit. She has been happily married to her husband and best friend, Justin, since 2008. Together they have two children, Ella and Gavin, who are her motivation, inspiration, and heart. In her spare time, Hope enjoys traveling, singing, cooking, reading books, working on wooden puzzles, spending time with friends and family, and relaxing.